PRAISE FOR
Messages from The Ancient Ones

"I've found that these short passages have created a needed and appreciated awareness about how I live my daily life. After reading a selection, I know how I can personally apply the information or respect and support those who are living a life that can more directly support the suggestions of The Ancient Ones. Thank you, Stacey Stephens, for giving the world these words of wisdom."
~ Carrie Louise, author of *Life, Soul Being Soul*

"Wherever you open this book it will speak to your heart and soul. Nourish yourself with this book as part of your spiritual practise." ~ Mary Llewellyn, Founding EFT Master

"With its short well-organized topics I found this book easy to digest, yet felt inspired to read on to the next topic and the next. The thought-provoking messages raised my awareness and acted as a gentle reminder for practices which I can become distracted from. I found this book to be positive and inspiring. A sense of reassurance that all is well and nothing needs to be sought after but rather to look within. I see this as a book that can be kept handy and dipped into at times of contemplation. Opening it up at any section will have a message that is relevant! I am pleased to have this in my book collection." ~ Marléne Rose Shaw, author of *Out Of Fear Into Love*

"If you're a fan of the Abraham/Esther Hicks channeled books, you will enjoy *Messages from the Ancient Ones* by Stacey Stephens. Well organized by topics such as Compassion, Empowerment, Relationships, Integrity, etc., the ideas presented are upbeat and almost utopian. If everyone took the advice to live by the ideals in this book, it would be a better place indeed.

I used the chapters as a daily devotional in the mornings. The messages are reminiscent of *A Course in Miracles*, talking about ego-based thinking and urging readers to breakthrough to an era of Divinity.

This book is part of the New Thought movement of spirituality. For those of us well-versed in this type of philosophy, it doesn't break new ground. However, it is a good presentation of the ideas and presents a hopeful image of what the human experience can be." ~ Dana Taylor, author of *Ever Flowing Streams*

"The Ancient Ones really 'spoke to me' on a level not many books do. Reading the words touched me physically as if a spark inside of me was recognised, acknowledged, held and understood. The messages shared within take you to a place where you are able to open your heart and mind; guiding us to a place where each of us becomes our true selves and in doing so raising the consciousness of all humanity.

Reading through you begin to understand how we show up in the world, how we influence others. Every one of us knowingly or unknowingly plays a role in the shift in consciousness around the world. The Ancient Ones teach us that acceptance is the key to gaining mastery in life, as is compassion, wisdom and service. It's up to us to make our mark in this time and space. Reading The Ancient Ones is simply a start to all you can be, for yourself, for others and for the world." ~ Wendy Fry, author of *Find YOU, Find LOVE*

Messages from The Ancient Ones

The First Five Years

Stacey Stephens

*Dedicated with gratitude to my loving husband
and Soul-mate, Jack, and my beautiful and
capable daughters, Cynthia and Alisha.*

Soul Self Living Publications
Reno, Nevada

MESSAGES FROM THE ANCIENT ONES:
THE FIRST FIVE YEARS

Copyright © Stacey Stephens, 2015

All Rights Reserved. No part of this book may be reproduced in any form, by photocopying or by any electronic, photographic or mechanical means, or in the form of a phonographic recording; nor may it be stored in a retrieval system, transmitted, or otherwise be copied for public or private use – other than for "fair use" as brief quotations embodied in articles and reviews - without prior permission in writing from both the copyright owner and the publisher.

The author of this book does not dispense medical advice or prescribe the use of any technique as a form of treatment for physical, emotional, or medical problems without the advice of a physician, either directly or indirectly. The intent of the author is only to offer information of a general nature to help you in your quest for emotional and spiritual well-being. In the event you use any of the information in this book for yourself, which is your constitutional right, the author and the publisher assume no responsibility for your actions.

First Published 2015 by
Soul Self Living Publications
(a division of Soul Self Living, Inc.)

www.SoulSelfLiving.com

Edited by Jack Stephens

ISBN: 0996407308
ISBN 13: 978-0-9964073-0-4

I wish to acknowledge The Ancient Ones for their clear and concise teachings of higher vibratory living. They have guided me throughout my life and shared with me great wisdom and compassion. I am grateful for their earnest desire to assist me, and all of mankind, to live a Soul Self life.

Contents

Foreword by The Ancient Ones xix
Preface by Stacey Stephens xxi
Introduction: The Ancient Ones xxiii

The Messages

Year One

    Humanity 1
    Divinity 1
    Creativity 2
    Interconnectedness 2
    Consciousness 3
    A Life Well Lived 5
    God 6
    Decide Your Life 7
    Healing 9
    Compassion 10
    Dignity 11
    Uncover Your Self 11
    Integrity 12
    Interdependence 12
    Relationships 13
    Soul Connection 14
    Perception 15
    Empowerment 16
    Children 17
    Youth 18

Soulmates	19
Family	20
Village	21
Global Society	22
Earth Ecology	23
Human Nature	24
Inner Calling	24
Purpose	25
Soul Authority	26
Oneness	27
Love	28
Being	29
Innocence	30
Reality	31
Passion	32
Attitude	33
Joy	34
Fulfillment	35
Belief	36
Wisdom	36
Image of God (1st Year Anniversary Message)	37

Year Two

Faith	41
Kindness	41
Patience	42
Inspiration	43
Spirit	44

Answers	44
Diversity	45
Positive Interpretation	46
Expression	47
Christmas	47
New Year	48
Mysticism	48
Bounty	50
Nature	50
Tolerance	51
Virtue	52
Experience	52
Harvest	53
Wholesomeness	54
Imagination	55
Upliftment	55
Allowing	56
Honoring	57
Co-Creating	57
Resurrection	58
Accountability	59
Earth	59
Question Relevance	60
Your Role	61
Mother's Day	61
Evolution vs. Tradition	61
Freedom	62

Highest Good 63

Conviction..64

Father's Day...64

Happiness 65

Manifesting 66

Life 67

Power..67

Contentment 68

Fun 69

Perspective...70

Enthusiasm 70

The Senses 71

Gratitude 72

Motivation 73

YOU 74

Pleasure 75

Designing Your Life 76

Action 76

Year Three

Cooperation 80

Assurance...80

Persistence 81

Community..81

Inner Guidance..82

Accord 83

Collaboration...84

Self-Responsibility 85

Example..86
Intention..86
Unconditional Love..87
Your Life's Garden 89
Empathy..91
Discernment..91
Equivalence...94
Mystical Mind 95
Signs of Nature...96
Help or Harm? 97
Back to Nature..98
Abundance..99
Ideas...100
Reincarnation 100
Activation of Blueprint 101
Create a Better Life 103
Make Your Voice Heard 103
Love or Fear..104
Change...105
Everything is Good..105
What Are You Afraid Of?...................................106
Mature Wisdom 107
Harvesting 108
Where Are You Creating From?........................109
Manifestation..110
Creatorship 111
Be Fertile Soil..111

    Positive Emotion 112
    Life Sustains Life 113
    Divine Expression 113
    Agreement 114
    Sociality 115
    God-Given Power 115
    Time 116
    True Power 117
    Activism 117
    Peace 118
    Play 119
    Connection 119
    Praise 120
    Experiential Living 120
    In Love 121
    Well-being 121

Year Four
    Creation 126
    Interpretation 126
    Congruence 127
    YOU Have Created Your Circumstance 128
    Free Yourself 129
    Worship 129
    Nutrition 130
    Natural Shelter 130
    Future 131
    Multidimensional 131

Resilience 132
Natural Teachers 132
Goodness 133
Healing Trauma 133
Love is Natural 134
Divine Ecstasy 135
Presence 135
Regenerative Sustainability 136
Honest Appraisal 136
Restoration 137
Caring for Animals 137
Food 138
Compassionate Listening 138
Transformation 139
Natural Living 139
Practical Spirituality 140
Allow 140
Manifest 141
Mother 141
Appreciation 142
Anticipation 142
Results 143
Group Consciousness 143
Father 144
Variety 144
True Joy 144
Share Love 145

Design or Default? 145

Now 146

Become the Change 146

Magic 147

Natural Order 147

Harmony 148

Believe 148

Positive Vibration 149

Who Says? 149

Do Not Judge 150

Make Better Choices 150

Heart Center 151

Year Five

Open Heart 155

Open the Flow 155

Body Temple 155

Simple Living 156

Thought Vibration 156

Self-Aware 157

Open Mind 158

Spiritual Guidance 158

Divine Being 159

Captivating 159

Your Well-being 160

Life is Good 160

Opportunity 161

God's Blessings 161

Joyful Expression	162
Move On	162
Improve Your Life	163
Start Again	164
Life's Diversity	164
Right to Choose	165
Wisdom is Experiential	165
Stay Connected	166
Natural Beauty	166
Begin with YOU	166
Open Your Heart	167
Re-Awaken Your Humanity	168
Family Unit	168
Soul Self	169
Nature's Example	169
God IS	169
Experience Happiness	170
Reverence	170
Organic Systems	171
Interdependent Sharing	171
True Sharing	171
Love Completely	172
Recharge	172
Become a Gift to the World	173
Good Vibes	173
Fairies	174
Loving Flow	174

Fellow Comrades 175

Are You A Mystic? 175

Healthy Designs 176

Procrastination 176

Soul Knowing 176

Pure Being 177

Heal Yourself 177

True Reality 178

Universal Light 178

Soul Sovereignty 178

Good Company 179

Afterword by The Ancient Ones 181

Foreword
The Ancient Ones

It is our desire to share with mankind a version of the world that is possible when people awaken their Souls from the slumber that has kept them inactive for so long.

The Soul is the pure power needed to change this life experience from a self-serving, ego-driven way of living to a Soul-centered way of Being.

WE are pleased to stimulate your Soul's awareness with the messages that we share each week. Encased in these five years of messages are valuable tidbits and stirrings for your Soul to uncover itself.

Utilize this information and bring these teachings deep within yourself to unlock your Soul's knowing. Act upon the wisdom to make the necessary changes in your own life, and to assist mankind into a more satisfying Soul-centered way of living.

Preface
Stacey Stephens

It has been my honor to work in collaboration with this very fine council who are lovingly known as, The Ancient Ones. The Ancient Ones also work within a larger council of which I am a part.

I have been in communication with them throughout my entire life. My earliest recollection of a disagreement is at about age six. It took me awhile to understand that they only desired my highest good. When I tried to tell my mother about them she denied that they were real. So, I continued learning from them and developing a strong trusting relationship in private.

They had told me that I was being prepared to act on their behalf to assist humanity to 'wake up' to their own divine nature. My part is to understand spiritual truth, speak out with courage, assist those interested, act on my guidance, and trust in the timing of everything.

The Ancient Ones have been helping me prepare my body to transmit Universal frequencies to awaken each person's individual Blueprint (their Soul's design for their current incarnation). When people become aware of their PURPOSE for this life, they will ignite their passion and become full participants in designing a greater expression of life.

The ego-mind has run rampant for too long. The ego is a tool for the Soul, as is the body. When our Soul is in charge of our life, with the mind and body in full cooperation, we will then know what it is to fully live. It is my true desire to assist humanity into this New Era of DIVINITY.

Introduction
The Ancient Ones

WE are eternal beings of non-physical form. WE make up a group of three, forming a council, for the guidance of Mankind, back to their original design as men and women. Our purpose is to assist everyone who is interested to develop their divine inner guidance, to direct themselves toward a humanity that is once again sacred and connected as One, in true camaraderie.

WE welcome you to an experience with us. It is our desire to awaken the divine blueprint within each individual person to become their unique and passionate expression as designed by themselves before entering into this particular incarnation during this specific time period on planet Earth.

There is no reason to restrict the expression of who you are. There is no 'judge' out there to punish or reward. There is only you and your fellow humans making judgments on each other. The ALL, or as many like to call it, GOD, is *all expression*. Higher levels of The ALL bring forth greater expressions of joy, love and peace. Yet, it is all acceptable in the experience within The ALL. You are at choice to express whatever level of consciousness you desire. Take charge of your personal life experience.

Join us in our vision of humanity coming together as ONE united people sharing Earth with all living forms in harmony and prosperity. WE will inform you of necessary changes for the evolution of mankind so you may make the shifts needed to bring forth the DIVINE PLAN that your Souls have agreed upon."

This World's Dilemma

We are aware of the many dilemmas facing humanity's continued existence. We would like to invite each individual to examine their way of living and make a conscious choice to change that which is not serving the whole of existence here on Earth.

We entreat you to have a greater role in raising the consciousness of the entire collective of humanity. Are you ready, willing and able to become the change you desire to experience on this planet? It all begins with YOU.

A Better Way

Many people are fed up with the way this ego-world is operated by leaders who do not consider the equivalence of all life. For centuries there have been power hungry rulers, fortune seeking commercial organizations, fanatically controlling religions, and self-aggrandized individuals whose consciousness is based upon separation and control over another.

There is a better way. When the authority of the Soul of each person is given credence, the direction of humanity will shift from oppressive ego-based fear into empowered unity of goodwill towards all.

The Game of this Ego-World

Have you noticed that there are several ways to look at a situation? Within the family unit, there is the point of view of the husband/father, wife/mother, eldest child, middle children, and the youngest, some with a male point of view and some with a female perspective. A family unit may also include extended family, such as grandparents, aunts, uncles, cousins, etc. Each person within the household will have their own ideas, agendas and desires. Who is right? How do you know what idea would work best for everyone involved?

Within a community there are many family units. Within a region there are many communities. Within a country there are numerous regions. And around the globe there are a number of countries. Humanity is a large group made up of individuals. Each person has his or her own desires. Each one is as important as the other. There is no rightful judge to proclaim sovereignty of one human over another.

Every rule or law is of man's making. These regulations are decided upon and enforced by man. No one can rightfully claim authority over another. The game is designed by human beings.

Think For Yourself

Are you aware that 99% of your thoughts have not originated from you? Since birth, most humans are indoctrinated with the thoughts held by their parents and caregivers. When a child enters school, they are taught to think the way of the accepted curriculum. A person's religious beliefs are usually adopted by their family's chosen religion. Political beliefs have been narrowed down within governments and offered as the only way. Even a person's thoughts concerning finances are entrained within them by the time they reach puberty.

For centuries adolescents have endeavored to change what they can see does not work or make sense, usually through rebellion or protest. There comes a point when many just give up and accept the lot they find themselves in. Many times this loss of personal power turns into depression, despair and even suicide.

The way things currently are can change. It takes fortitude to withstand the opposing forces of the already existing ego-world. Tradition can only continue if people choose to perpetuate it. Take your stand on what you personally agree with. Replace what does not work with something better. Take the time to ponder the many questions that bubble forth within your mind. Think a new thought, if you dare.

What would that look like? Nobody can say. New thoughts do not have a past. Innovations come to those willing to think outside the limitations of past knowledge. How many original thoughts have you had in the span of your lifetime? Make sure they are truly original and not just knockoffs of someone else's idea. Your honest reflection may be startling, indeed.

Most changes made in this ego-world are just slightly different calibers, degrees, or variations of the existing plan. Nothing completely new is ever received with ease. There is usually commercial 'red tape,' political agendas and religious opposition that must be dealt with before anything new can be permitted. This ego-world's commercial, political and religious factions must first accept a new idea before it can be implemented.

With seven billion people living together on Earth, change can take place more quickly if people would take responsibility to come together as a united group to insist that peace replace war, tolerance replace racism, equivalence replace hierarchy, honesty replace deception, honor replace inhuman treatment, shelter, food and clothing be provided to replace poverty, medical treatment be offered freely to replace undue illness, basic education for all to replace illiteracy, preservation of nature to replace destruction to our Earth, and forward-moving evolution to replace stagnant, man-made tradition.

It is in your hands as human beings to make the necessary changes to preserve the future of humanity. Your ideas are important. Think for yourselves. Find those of like mind to form the needed mass consciousness to create the changes you desire. Do your part to improve the living conditions for all of Earth's inhabitants. Your future is dependent on making extreme changes to shift from this ego-based world to a Soul-based world. What new thoughts can you share?

Join Together

Co-creation together as a united humanity will ensure the changes you desire. There are already groups forming around the globe to encourage people's involvement in creating a better future for every living creature on Earth. Sift through the groups and find one that speaks your passion. Join forces to enhance the movement and give of your time and energy to promote your cause.

Replace your compliant inactivity with passionate action. Make a difference in this world. Become involved with like-minded people to create a new future. Instead of complaining about or ignoring the problems of harmful environmental destruction, use your voice to alert others of the necessary changes that must take place in order to support an environment that supports ALL life.

When everyone becomes accountable for Earth's well-being, you will see mass improvement. Get involved somehow. Take your place among your brothers and sisters. Unite together to bring peace, harmony and love to this world's affairs.

You are what you have been waiting for, so STOP WAITING!

Equitable Economy

Humans have devised a world based upon inequitable economy. Would it not make more sense to create a governing system that provides the bare necessities of life, including housing, food, water, clothing and medical treatment? Leaving room for those who choose to upgrade for a cost? This would eliminate poverty, while still giving everyone the opportunity to improve their circumstances as they desire.

How can this world survive in its current state of affairs? Too many inhabitants are left to die of starvation, sickness and poverty. Where is the camaraderie? Where is the fellow feeling? Where is the Oneness?

Reach deep within yourself to find your humanity. Become the type of person that looks out for all of God's creatures. Play a larger role in the shift in consciousness that is building momentum as people are awakening to the understanding that this world is made up of ideas that have been implemented by their predecessors and can easily be changed by those who are currently living here on Earth.

Break with tradition and choose a better way! It is up to YOU.

Deck of Cards

Let us use the analogy of a deck of playing cards to express how people can be viewed as living in differing levels of consciousness. You have 52 playing cards, plus two Jokers. See each one as the numeral value of the card, with Aces as highest value and Jokers as least value. The number cards are in the learning process, the face cards have mastered certain higher principles, the Aces have reached wholeness from which to teach, and the Jokers have left the game all together. Yet, the Jokers remain to provide powerful contrast from which others may make a choice: whether to follow these anti-lifers or the holistic teachers.

    Ace – Holistic Master Teacher
    Jack, Queen & King – Developing Master
    2 – 10 – Novice
    Joker – Anti-life Contraster

    We offer this analogy not as a tool for judgment, for there is equivalence in all life. Rather, it is a fun way to choose which cards you want to hold in your hand. Everyone is part of THE ALL, yet each one expresses at differing levels of consciousness. Eventually each one will make it to the level of wholeness. And, choosing wisely whom you associate with will help you to build your strength.

    Acceptance is a key to gaining mastery in life, as is compassion, wisdom, and service.

    The Jokers are the ones to avoid if you desire to win with your hand of cards, so discard them immediately when they show up in your hand, for they will do their best to pull you off course from your purpose. They feed on the energy of other people and they interfere by usurping another's inner authority. They play with guilt, shame, judgment, and condemnation. They live in fear of life, naming Self-expression as bad. They control through manipulation by means of bullying, seduction, and/or puritanical condemnation. Watch out for these false cards!

We hope you have enjoyed our fun. And, remember, the game never ends, so find as much joy as you can while playing your hand.

Shift Your Perception

Allow us to adjust your perception. Similar to when the Earth was proven to be round and not flat. Are you willing to look at things differently than you were taught?

Many people still believe that God is a personage, a male figure in the sky proclaiming judgment on evil-doers. This however, does not make logical sense when it comes to the examination of consciousness, the Oneness of the Universe, or the newer scientific understandings about Quantum Physics.

Logically, it makes better sense to perceive God as ALL THAT IS. This validates the religious sanctions of God's omni qualities. And, scientifically, we are all made from the same substance – ENERGY. Can you fathom God as the sea of energy that makes up Universes? Energy is information. Consciousness has intelligence. Can you think of God as the intelligence that makes up consciousness?

If you are able to experience God in a broader way, without the limitations of a humanized Deity, you will find that all of the laws made in God's name are actually man's laws. They are opinions of men claiming false authority over your individual right to believe as you choose. These rule makers demand your obedience and utilize punishment for offenders.

It is time for each person to find their own inner truth, their inner knowing, and release themselves from the bondage of these man-made false beliefs disguised as "God's Way." Open your minds and hearts to your true inner voice and live in compassionate co-existence with all of life.

A New World

Yes, change is necessary. From our perspective, it is easier than you think. Fear prevents people from taking action. Courage overcomes fearful paralysis. Raise your consciousness above the fear-based ego dominance of this world, and look within to your Soul's courageous strength and conviction. With your Soul's guidance you can overcome every imagined fear and become the REAL, whole, wise, powerful, fully aligned human being that you are.

It will take REAL HUMAN BEINGS to co-create a united world of peace and prosperity for ALL.

Open Your Heart

Move beyond the syrupy sentimentality that many have named, 'love.' This gushy mentality uses manipulative fear-based control mechanisms to guilt, shame, and coerce people to conform to a rule-based institutionalized way of living with the false pretense of promoting peace.

There is no peace within the constrictions of the human spirit. Conformity creates death. We mean to say that constricting the flow of life-force energy leads to illness and dis-ease, and eventually the loss of the will to live.

To slow down evolution, and gain control, certain institutions have developed a sly way of misleading the masses into a complacent, almost non-existence. We are here to help awaken within each individual their divine right to co-create a world for the betterment of ALL, not just a few who place themselves as superior to the rest.

The time is NOW to open your hearts to the truth of your inner knowing, your Soul's agenda. Yes, that's right! Your Soul has an agenda, both personal and universal. Awaken to your higher knowing and allow this empowering wisdom to assist you in standing up for your personal divine right as a living entity in human form here on planet Earth. And, join with your fellow brothers and sisters around the globe to co-create the life that your Souls have agreed upon before you incarnated.

Wake up from the slumber that this ego-dominated world has put you in. Take charge of your life, and participate with humanity to overthrow the prison of your mind. Become an activist for a future where life is celebrated, real love is shared, and individuality is encouraged within the entirety of the whole.

True expression is found within your heart. Open wide.

The Answer is Inside of You

Everything you need to know is inside of you, connected to your Soul's knowing. Reach deep within to the silence and then wait patiently for the answer to your question to appear. It may come through in the still small voice, it may be seen in a vision, or perhaps a prophetic dream while you sleep. The answer will make itself known one way or another. Expect it, and yet remain patient until you have the 'aha' experience.

Prophets of old were not the only ones to receive messages. Everyone is capable of experiencing revelations. Find your Soul's voice, and utilize the great wisdom it has to offer. Your Soul is aware of so much more than your ego-mind or body could ever understand. Become well acquainted with your higher knowing and rely upon its unfailing guidance. Your Soul is, after all, your truest friend.

Year One

Humanity

Humans were designed originally to co-create with each other new and exciting experiences, for a greater sharing and connection of their divinity. Each human being is equipped with an internal guidance system that allows them to uncover wisdom from within each new adventure. The collective consciousness therefore, can grow at an exceedingly rapid pace when shared from the Soul Space or heart.

Wholesome goodness or destructive separation can run through the minds of people depending on the consciousness of the sender. This is why it is vital to dismantle the ill-making belief systems that are rampant in today's world. Soul to Soul connection prevents the lesser elements from taking hold, and thereby offers a much higher vibration of cooperation, harmony and love.

Sharing from divinity encourages progress toward a greater humanity.

Divinity

The concept of divinity is the awareness of each human's personal authority over their creation, that is, over their life. Whether designing life from wisdom or folly, each one is solely responsible for what shows up (or not) in their own experience. The Soul's wisdom is a valiant guide to creating an inspiring and useful life. The ego, on the other hand, can create divisions and competition due to its limited ability to care beyond one's own person.

Creating from divinity means accepting full responsibility for oneself, and for everyone and everything that may be affected by one's actions. Responsible humans endeavor to create an environment where all can express from their individual creativity, while also sharing with the whole of humanity the fundamental needs of the collective.

Creativity

To create is the purpose of all beings. Each person automatically creates from every thought and feeling that are combined. This is why thinking positive thoughts and feeling positive emotions are necessary for creating positive outcomes. Attention is needed to tend to the proper creations in order to bring forth desirable results. It is also necessary to abandon harmful ways so that there will be no delays or obstructions to ones desires. Consciousness creates through thought and feeling, so it is up to each one to be diligent in themselves to create peace, harmony and love for all of humanity.

It is the Soul of each individual that is concerned with the well-being of all. An ego-driven world concerns itself with power, prestige and profit. To create a world where all of humanity can share with all of Nature in cooperation, harmony and peace, people will need to raise their consciousness to the level of the Soul, where wisdom and unconditional love abide.

Because human beings create all before it appears in materialized form, they should be able to know in advance the makings of their minds. They can use their ability to "see" their future endeavors coming into fruition for everything, including their health, wealth and relationships. One must remove all negative thought patterns by disowning them. Realizing that time is fluid, it will therefore come according to each individual's conviction. And, it can be sped up with certainty.

Interconnectedness

Mankind is awakening into the era of divinity. The human race is opening to spiritual understanding. In this time of evolution, people are breaking free from the control inflicted by ego consciousness. No longer will those who have awakened accept authority outside of themselves. Divinity requires Soul authority. The Soul is aware of the interconnectedness that is Spirit, non-physical.

The collapse of outer authority is upon us. We have entered the era of co-creation, as individual incarnations living for God, or the all of us. It is only a matter of time before consciousness reaches the level of interconnectedness where each living Soul is seen and felt as a part of ourselves, thereby caring for the other as oneself. Full realization will bring unity.

There are many levels within the matrix of consciousness. Earth is supportive of a multitude of levels. As humanity awakens further into the interconnectedness of the all, the lesser levels of understanding based upon false concepts of separation will diminish. Humanity's Soul recognition automatically overcomes, or evolves ignorance. Every human is capable of raising their level of consciousness into the more accurate understanding of universal existence. There is no separation. This is a misconception based upon ignorance. "We are all one" is a universal concept known by all that has been forgotten but not lost. Divinity is inevitable because it is reality.

Consciousness

It is All *God*. Consciousness holds within itself every level conceivable to the human mind and then some. Just because one does not understand the simplicity of life, love, and ultimately GOD does not mean that it is not reality. Life *is*, love *is*, and God *is*. Simply put, there is nothing that is outside of *God*. Judgment sets things outside of the truth that nothing can or ever will be separated from The *ALL* of existence. Therefore, any idea that suggests separation is based on falsehood.

Religion can bring people closer to their inner knowing that *love* is the way to happiness. Yet, because of the divisions made by the people who ignorantly reject their fellow man, love becomes a word rather than a way of life. To love another is to accept their choice to live and believe whatever they choose. It does not mean that you have to agree with them or do as they do, but rather it is just to accept their personal choice while making up your own mind to choose for yourself.

Diversity is God's greatest gift. Acceptance is man's greatest attribute. Discernment allows one to accept for another while deciding differently for oneself. There is no judgment in true discernment. Practice using discernment for yourself while accepting someone else's different choice for them as alright and you will find a great peace come over you erasing the anxiety created by judgment.

You will no longer fear punishment by an angry entity when you raise your awareness to a height that dispels all false notions of judgment. Karma is simply experiencing the consequences of your own choices, whether made in ignorance or with full knowledge. Pardon comes from the *Self* when understanding occurs and forgiveness is exercised. It is all within you, for you are made in the image and likeness of The *All*, or *God*.

The time has come for a greater understanding of Reality to unfold. No more separation. Endeavor to see everything in the frame of *Oneness*. See everyone as an individuation of the *One*. Choose for yourself your own way. Honor each person's right to choose for themselves.

No harm can come to you without your participation in the equation. Remember that this is not the only incarnation you have ever experienced. The show goes on and on. Everything in your life is drawn to you from your former level of consciousness which directed your choices. Shift yourself to higher levels of consciousness so you can make better choices and you will find the recipe to change for the better. Change your perception on a daily basis to better fit your grander idea of yourself.

We are all *One*. Whether in body or not, we are all made of the same substance which is *God*. Be God now. You already are. Yet there is so much more expression that you are capable of as you accept your own Divinity.

Humanity is waking up to the truth of their being. Who do you want to *be*?

A Life Well Lived

It is with great wonder that a child finds him or herself as a part of the human race. When they are guided lightly and encouraged to explore what they find as their delight, they often will achieve remarkable feats due to their unlimited imagination. No one has yet squelched their enthusiasm or controlled their thinking. Jesus said that one must be as a little child in order to understand the ways of God. Open your mind to experience more than you were taught and allow children to expand their knowledge through experimentation and inner listening. They still have a great deal of humility and are not yet "know-it-alls".

Time is available for people to experience all kinds of ways of living. Search for yourself what you would prefer to create as your life. When you are sure of your choice, then *go for it!* This expenditure of energy will ignite more passion as you see and feel the results of your desire. Joy will be a natural by-product of your quest. This is true living.

Be daring! When you do not need the approval of others, when you do not have to dampen your enthusiasm to avoid offending another, when you no longer buy into the false idea of a wrathful deity, then you can soar above the clouds of old ideas, and you can run past the antiquated ways of tradition. Find your passion and begin to fully live the life of your choosing. It is up to you to feel your truth, to decide your future and then to act on your inner guidance to bring it about for yourself.

Your innate nature is good. Trust your desire for everyone else to experience happiness. Competition is a learned practice. Scarcity is a misinterpretation of the proper formula, which is circulation. As long as there is circulation there is no lack. Fear causes a slowing down of the flow, greed creates a hording and stops the flow, but keeping the flow going will overcome the dilemma of lack. For example, to continue building houses from wood one must replant the trees in order to have the resources for the next allotment of houses. To continue anything one must replenish that which has been used. This is circulation.

Exercise your inner knowing. Practice listening to your true desires. Take the time necessary to get to know yourself, your likes and what ignites your passion. Make the needed changes in your circumstances that will bring you more joy and fulfillment in your life. Take responsibility for designing the life that you truly desire to live. It is all up to you. Begin now and continue each and every day. What is your idea of a life well lived? Decide, and then *go for it!*

God

To be happy and fulfilled one needs only to love. Sharing love with another is also necessary for true wholeness in life. Either fear or judgment is indicative of a life cut off from Reality which is *Love*. No one can cut off your flow of life, love or Divinity. It is always an inside job. When love is withheld, it is only one-sided, unless the one being slighted takes part in the deprivation. This is the secret to enduring joy – never stop the flow of love from pulsating within you, even when the person outside of you is restricting their involvement.

Love is ever present. Life, love, Divinity, energy, consciousness, these are interchangeable words depicting the same inference to God. Nature is also another word simulating God's role as life bringer and sustainer. Do not get caught up in the meaning of words. Accept that *all* is God.

The many levels and layers of God can be felt wherever you are in your current understanding of life. Tolerance of another's concept of The *All* is most beneficial. And, acceptance is even better. Who has the authority to deny another of their personal concept of God? There is much more to the definition than can ever be described in words. Accept that the depth shall always be more than the observance.

Create your ideas from within your *Self* and you shall know better than most that God is *everything*. Who can separate God from anything? Presumptuousness is foolhardy. There is no place found in all of existence where life is nonexistent. This can only mean one thing, *life* is God. How you choose to live your God-given life is up to you and no other.

We hope you will awaken to your full knowing that you are all a part of the whole, that is – you are all God as well as the plants and animal life. Take care of your fellow brothers and sisters because there is no separation in the whole of existence which is God.

Decide Your Life

It is with great care that one should choose their actions, for it is in the deciding that energy is set in motion. To think of the outcome and foresee the eventual consequences is wisdom. All decisions lead to actions, whether in the personal arena or if acted out by the collective. Spirit directs the completion of a person's choices. Default circumstances occur when one is incomplete with their desires or fails to take proactive steps to fulfill their dreams.

Your life is by your design as soon as you are able to choose for yourself your attitude and actions. Until then, it is in the hands of whomever you allow to govern your life. Learn to think things through to completion, so you will be in charge of your creations. When one is lazy in their designing process they tend to reap seemingly undesirable results. It is all in your own hands to create your future. Take the time to ponder your future and choose wisely that which will bring about the desired outcome. Wake up to the knowing that if you take full responsibility in your decision making process you will be the master creator of your life. It is never too late to start.

Begin with your awareness that illness is a problem with the flow of life-force energy throughout your body. Removal of negative thought programs will automatically reverse most ailments. Think of health as streams of light flowing through your veins enlivening every cell to accomplish its purpose. When a dam is formed the flow stops and those parts of the body are no longer receiving their needed share of the life-force that keeps them in good operation.

Illness can be prevented or healed by allowing the life-force energy to flourish. Love, joy and true desire awaken the flow within. Negative thought forms or programs restrict this life-affirming flow. Seek to overcome your judgments by transforming them into positive interpretations. For instance, racism can be transformed by viewing beauty and diversity within the human race, as similar to the beauty and diversity among Earth's flowers, which can bring such pleasure to the senses. Drug addicts can be seen as people seeking to feel good, though by ignorant means. When light, love, and compassion are shown towards people who bring harm to themselves, many are able to see the folly of their ways, and improve their circumstances with the assistance of those in better living conditions. Condemnation helps no one. Offer a helping hand to those who desire to choose higher ways. Show them their Divine nature, and demonstrate to them their very own personal power to change themselves for the better, so they can create the life that they desire.

Compassion is to understand that while people innately desire to live a happy life, many are overcome with false thinking based upon separation from the whole of existence. Come back to your inner knowing that everyone is a component of the whole. Uplift those who fall down in their ways. Encourage everyone to choose Peace. Show by example how unconditional love is master over judgment. True service overcomes selfishness. Desiring joy for all opens the way for camaraderie. And, responsible decision making is key to creating a better life for oneself. What do you desire to experience? When you have figured that out, decide and do your part to bring it about by proper action.

Healing

Life is renewed as long as the body remains in the flow of life-force energy. Restricted energy flow begins the illness process due to lack of proper nutrients nourishing the cellular structures. True health is supported by proper nutrition, living water, adequate shelter, enough sleep, physical exercise, joyful expression and real love.

Allowing oneself to be happy is a cure-all formula. Joy is the greatest elixir for life. Passion moves energy throughout the physical body better than a five mile run or a one-hour aerobic workout. Passion fuels the entire Self, not just the physical body.

Health is more than a strong physical body. It is a joyful, passionate expression of life as you. Divinity is pure energy, ultimate consciousness, it is life-force. It IS, and it flows wherever there is no resistance. Like water that flows downstream until it merges into the ocean, only stopping due to anything blocking its way, so too life-force energy enlivens everything that has the proper channels.

When someone becomes ill due to long-term improper food intake, they are able to remedy the problem quite well by changing and enhancing their diet. When someone injures their body, incurring a broken bone, with sufficient rest the bone will mend itself. When a person is ill from emotional trauma, love, patience and encouragement from friends work wonders in bringing back the patients desire to live and that is when healing really takes place.

Humans are more than bodies and minds. The whole person must be taken into account. With Soul involved one can perceive life from a higher perspective, where unity abides. Divinity is living life as a whole person, body/mind/Soul. To separate any aspect from the whole is ignorance at work.

Energy channels within the body matrix can easily be unblocked with greater awareness of life and how it operates. Life flows until it is blocked. By keeping your Self flowing with love, there will be no blockage to cause illness. Judgment and condemnation create blocks within the one holding to the improper thought patterns. Love, acceptance, allowance and Self-responsibility through discernment can keep the flow of love pulsating throughout the entire body, while encouraging the other to move into love by example. This way of invitation honors another's path and learning process. The answer is love.

Love your Self to health. Love others, and assist them to heal by invitation. Allow each person to come into their own knowing that *love* is synonymous with *life, energy* and *God*.

Compassion

Acceptance of another's belief shows compassion without having the same opinion. Allowing someone to choose for themselves their way of life is showing compassion without agreement. Honoring a person's right to decide for themselves is a compassionate gesture that evokes trust in the process of life where learning comes in many forms, sometimes through trial and error.

Compassion understands that there is nothing in this world that can separate one from God, ALL THAT IS. No person, place or thing is separate from The ALL of existence. There are only varying degrees of life, love, Spirit.

Playing judge is the idle occupation of ignorance. Discernment is nonjudgmental. It is only concerned with whether something is of true value for oneself without the condemnation involved. To condemn anyone, or anything for that matter, is a sign of ignorance. To discern what is right for oneself is wisdom. Accept and allow others to choose for them. Honor their divine right to make mistakes and learn. Pay attention to yourself and mind your own business.

The *ALL* allows, honors and accepts everything. God is *Love*. God is *Life*. God *Is*, no exception.

Dignity

Dignity is a sense of pride, self-esteem and self-respect. A person's dignity cannot be removed by another. It is self-judgment, condemnation and guilt that degrade oneself. When a human acts from integrity, although there may be others who believe his actions to be wrong, if he himself knows that his action is pure he keeps his sense of pride. On the other hand, when he behaves in a manner that goes against his inner wisdom he may diminish his self-esteem with a sense of shame. Once he has remedied the situation and brought himself back into integrity he regains his self-respect.

Keep your dignity by keeping your own counsel. Seek your answers from within yourself. Gain clarity from an inner dialog with your divine guidance system before making decisions. Act on your Soul's direction and you will build a strong empowered sense of Self.

Uncover Your Self

Within your Self is a state of being that is authentic. This natural embodiment within yourself speaks to you with quiet whispers, it shows you visions within your imagination, it shares with you direction through feelings. When you feel joy, love, peace, passion or expansiveness this is your guidance telling you that you are on the right track. When you feel negativity, uneasiness or constriction this is yourself prodding you to find another way.

Intuition is innate within all forms of life. Listen to your hunches and "gut feelings". Valuable information is being shared at all times. Learn to listen and dialog. Clarity comes from developing a solid communication with your Soul. You are the most important person in your life. Cultivate trust and uncover your core. Build your character through integrity to you, your true self, your Soul Self.

You are here on Earth for a number of reasons. Find out what they are so you can fulfill your purpose. Spend time alone in contemplation, commune with your Soul through daily meditation. Become your own best friend. Uncover the mystical, magical expression that is uniquely YOU.

Integrity

Integrity to oneself, one's own Soul is the highest form of integrity. It takes courage to be honest and to honor one's true direction. False loyalty to another has been the downfall of many. Humans are never required to give up their integrity to their own truth for any reason. Sentimentality can be used as a tool to manipulate and control people. Become aware of these subtle tactics which can rob one of self-empowerment.

You are responsible to yourself. Check within before deciding to take action. This is your life to live. Be wise and choose life affirming actions. Apply yourself to develop your divine inner guidance system and to build your self-esteem and integrity.

Interdependence

We are designed to share with one another in an interdependent manner. This innate knowing within all human beings and nonphysical entities alike can be awakened with understanding in the unity of the WHOLE. There is nothing set apart from The ALL, nothing. Grasping this will not only open one to acknowledge everything as a piece and parcel of God, but it will even take one further into enlightenment with the comprehension that everything IS, without exception, God.

With this concept understood, mankind can regain their sense of camaraderie and move away from the false teachings of judgment and condemnation. And rather, utilize their own discernment for their individual lives. This in and of itself will diminish separation and superiority among humankind.

It is our desire to elevate people's awareness to a more accurate understanding of how consciousness creates their world. There is nothing outside of yourself that has more power in your life experience than YOU. Each individual creates, accepts, allows or resists anything and everything from coming into their own experience. If you are lacking it is because you hold lack in your belief system. If you are building success it is because you are accepting it within your belief. Search within to find where in your thoughts, feelings and beliefs these issues or abilities exist. Change that which does not bring you your desired result. It is all up to you to create your personal experience on planet Earth. Look within.

Relationships

We, as a consciously aware group, both in body and non-physical form, communicate at all times with the present level of consciousness in any given moment. Words are a small portion of relating with another, gestures even smaller. Actions may be loud, but energy, or PRESENCE, is even a greater force that is felt by all.

You cannot hide your consciousness behind a mask for very long. Time reveals the accuracy of your state of consciousness. There is no way to convince someone of your intention if your energy does not match your words or actions. Lies can be felt quite easily when you are clear enough within yourself to distinguish between the energies.

We are entering a time when people are becoming more tuned in to themselves through their intuition and inner-feeling guidance system. There will be little room left for the "con", when society awakens to their innate knowing. It is just a matter of time before the world of humanity, once again, opens its doors to good, old-fashioned common sense and intuition.

Choosing wisely for oneself will again become the natural state of each individual. This will unite all who are honest and inspired to build their future with those of like mind and open heart. Community will prevail once more, and the camaraderie of all will create a unity of peace, trust, acceptance, respect and love.

Soulmates will be drawn to each other without the interference of the misguided ego drama. Families will build their future with dignity based on respect for individuality and full self- expression. Spiritual communities will be founded upon diversity and the celebration of life.

Become your true identity, your Soul Self, and join with others to create a world of joyful expression, of laughter and love, of divinity in human form.

Soul Connection

It is with pleasure that we assist humanity to reconnect with each other, Soul to Soul. This means one is authentic and with pure intention (not to "get" something from another). Think deeply about this concept. When you communicate with anyone, is there a motive behind it to serve yourself? If there was nothing in it for you, would you take the time or make the effort? How self-serving are you? It may disturb you to see just how ego-driven you are behaving.

To connect with another, just for the sake of sharing love, life and friendship, means that you are both complete in the exchange, with nothing further needing to take place when the connection is finished. Nothing is expected from the other. Sharing from a Soul position is, in itself, the "be all". How many of these experiences do you share in a day, a week, a month?

It is easy to shift your focus from "getting" to SHARING. Try it often throughout your week and experience the joy and fulfillment that it brings to you and your companions. Experience the satisfaction derived from authentically giving of yourself to another. Feel the trust that emerges from this new way of being with another. See for yourself the true relationships that develop over extended periods of time, sharing Soul to Soul. Watch your life become a manifestation of fruitful connections and experiences of true relating.

Perception

Consciousness is life expressing in differing degrees. Life ever exists in one stage or another, as demonstrated within the "circle of life". Everything is energy, and it is everywhere. There is no place without God. God is ALL THAT IS, and all that seems not.

With this awareness comes maturity, wisdom and acceptance, so that judgment no longer holds sway. Personal discernment replaces judgment of another. Freedom to live for and as one's true Self thrives. The joy of creating one's own adventure becomes the foundation for true expression. Life then opens to meaning, purpose and passion.

Many spiritual teachers have expressed these wisdom teachings of non-judgment, love without conditions, fulfillment of true desire, reaping that which is sown, and unity with all of life. Humanity's innate nature is positive. The Soul's direction is always to deliver that which can be utilized for positive change.

It is the misunderstanding of the ego-mind that has created false judgments to be written and agreed upon by the masses. Belief can only look real in the eye of the beholder. When one changes their way of seeing, that is, their perception, a different belief is born, and circumstances change to support that new belief. Yet, in reality, nothing really claims TRUTH because it is all based on bias.

Gaining a higher perspective usually unravels the belief below it. So, to get ahead of the game, one can simply release their sense of "rightness" or judgment and, instead, keep an open mind to the ever-expanding awareness of reality and the meaning of life, and therefore truly enjoy the process of becoming.

Your beliefs are the only things hindering you from truly being happy. Choose to interpret your life experience from the viewpoint that everything is happening for your good. Look deep within yourself to see that whatever you are going through is somehow related to your current level of awareness or belief. If you are experiencing that which you do not desire, then find the belief that is creating it (in obedience to your belief pattern) and change your perception to create a different outcome.

There is no one out there in the ethers punishing you for anything you have done in your past. There is only YOU creating your circumstances from your interpretation or belief system. Mankind has created all kinds of deities for the purpose of punishing, rewarding, and controlling their fellow man. It is time to awaken from your shared creation of a world based on false premises of separation from The *ALL*, and the concept of "good versus evil".

Life is an unending journey of enjoyment. The Soul enjoys sharing with others. Relating with another brings fulfillment. No human stands alone, for one cannot exist without connection to all of life.

Each individual is their own authority as their divinely-inspired Soul Self, and, at the same time, connected to everyone and everything. Open your awareness to greater levels of perception, find the positive interpretation of your circumstances, and experience the natural result of empowered, joyful living in unity with the whole of LIFE.

Empowerment

We are all the same. Each entity, whether plant, animal, human or Spirit, are made up of the same substance, which is identified as consciousness. We each carry within ourselves a distinction called personality. Therefore, we are all equal "brothers and sisters" in a world made of communication through energetic connection. Every day we relate with each other continuously whether we are aware of it or not.

When this understanding is awakened within us, we have the opportunity to excel in our expansion. Life is meant to be a journey of joyful exploration and Self-empowerment. Many universal teachings repeat the knowing that "we are all one." This knowing is felt deep within the psyche and clear through to the bones, so to speak. Nothing can truly explain the depth of our connection and so we must allow ourselves to move forward with just an inkling of perceived understanding until we are standing in it, BEING it.

Until then, we can accept our Divinity through the filters of unworthiness, realizing that we can, at any moment, accept a higher truth about our nature. We are on an upward spiral leading to Self-Realization. Nothing can prevent us from attaining that which is REAL.

Experiencing love for ourselves, and love for our fellow beings, every living entity, will awaken our deep knowing of interconnectedness, ONENESS.

Children

Like other mammals, humans care for their young until they are capable of caring for themselves. The fox teaches their young to hunt, and other skills that are needed to perpetuate their kind. And, when their offspring are ready they are booted from the warmth of their mother's den, expected to fend for themselves.

A natural, intact society raises their children within this natural framework. Their young are taught how to feed, shelter, and clothe themselves, and to care for future families of their own. They learn skills and trades that express their passions, with the opportunity of mastery as they apply themselves. Each child grows to become a useful citizen within their community, able to contribute to the continuation of the people.

Entitlement is not taught, nor is it tolerated. Each member of society is expected, and honored, to do their part. Positive pride is encouraged and developed within each individual. Service is a sign of well-being. Youth are treated with dignity and given opportunities to carry their own load. A sense of belonging is cultivated. No one is left behind. There is work for all to contribute to the common good.

We are coming back to this natural state of being, back to grassroots community. It is time to take pride in our capableness as a human race to live in integrity to oneself, and in community with others. Life is simple when the distractions of the ego world are removed. Are you ready?

Youth

It is a fascinating experience to move from childhood to adulthood. In between the two comes a very awkward stage of development known as adolescence. Within this period of time, a youth has the opportunity to step out on his or her own, to decipher for themselves what they choose to accept in belief or action. Many times this stage brings with it harsh judgments from both adults and fellow peers. How does one stand firm, with resolve, to choose for themselves a way of expression that is right for them, even sometimes against all odds?

How many young adults are truly thinking for themselves? How many people, for that matter, are keeping their own counsel? Do you have the faith and courage to listen within to the directives of your Soul? Can you stand firm in your integrity amidst a myriad of opinions? Do you have the strength and diligence to show others a new way?

We are each endowed with whatever we need to know to make a wise decision. We all have our inner guidance from our Soul to show us our individual path. Everyone is capable of listening within and contemplating their own choices, their own direction. We need only remove the blinders from our eyes; the massive bombardment of society's regulated codes of conduct that are crippling to one's true nature.

Each young person is completely able to break free from the constraints of this antiquated way of living, to explore for themselves a higher pathway, a greater expression of life, a more fulfilled way of being. Choose now to develop your divinely-authored good sense. And, show mankind the way through the current mess of ego domination, into the era of Soul inspired, co-creative participation in human living.

Soulmates

Like other mammals, humans are created male and female. And, like some, we are designed to pair together to raise our young. Along with caring for children, we have an opportunity to provide heritage by co-creating our future with purpose.

Peace and fulfillment are the natural result of a harmonious match. Soulmates can create a successful union, acting as king and queen of their realm. Stronger still, one Soul divided into two incarnations (one male, and the other female) is a partnership that creates a united kingdom that cannot be divided.

Each successful coupling is a gift to mankind. With true partnership there is ease in the relationship, and longevity in their mission together. Each time a couple unites in LOVE and purpose, they open the way for humanity to reawaken their true design of Soul sovereignty, Soulmate union, strong family, grassroots community, and world-wide connection.

Proper partnership eliminates trauma created by separation, divorce, broken homes, and neglected children. It creates a strong value system based on integrity to SELF first, then mate, children, community and finally, global family.

Each time a true partnership is made, a powerful energy emerges. This higher frequency also lifts others up to experience greater fulfillment. Each successful union strengthens the growing wave of people searching for their Soulmate. And, in time, humanity will experience a deeper sense of belonging, and a richer connection with everyone.

Family

The desire to create a family is one of the most basic expressions of humanity. Most people retain their innate nature to procreate. It is a natural part of being human.

The need to continue the species is only a fraction of the pull we feel to connect and proliferate. Deeper in our psyche is a need to create kinship, a bond that will fulfill the needs of being human. These include trust, belonging, affection, companionship, nurturing, child rearing, and the continuation of our lineage, to name a few.

Involvement in this natural expression brings satisfaction. Every living being on this bountiful Earth is drawn to participate, in one form or another, in the creation of family. Nothing can truly take the place of this natural occurrence.

It is this longing to fulfill our nature that continues humanity. Without this natural expression the world of humankind would cease. The Earth would become void of the intelligence to co-create a harmonious world, and to connect as a global family.

This can never come to pass as long as there are men and women alive and willing to keep us moving forward. Recognize this need within yourself, and ask how you can participate in the growth and continuation of humanity, bringing forward this strong family unit as a focal point once again.

Village

A village is a community of families who grow together through generations. Each person born is welcomed within both their family and tribe. As the young ones mature, they are encouraged to discover themselves, and find their special niche that assists their people to evolve and prosper.

As the community members work together to co-create unity within diversity, they are able to produce an atmosphere where dignity and service are cultivated. This creates a sense of camaraderie, belonging, and united purpose. With respect for each member, the village can multiply and thrive.

We are coming back to an era of grassroots community, with a focus on the well-being of the individual within the group. Both of these aspects of communal living are very important for the assurance of a fulfilling life. Individual sovereignty and the needs of the village are valued and honored for the sense of fellowship and wholeness they create.

The natural human being is returning. The individual is reclaiming sovereignty, placing great value on proper matches and strong, supportive families, rebuilding intact communities, and recognizing the interconnectedness of all living beings around the globe.

Where are you currently in your interactions with others? Are you expressing your true voice as your authentic Self? Are you joined together with a harmonious partner? Are you raising a strong family? Are you involved within your community as an active participant? Are you treating everyone on Earth as an extended family member?

Choose now to develop yourself into a capable and valued member of society. Find your strengths, develop your virtues, and fulfill your true desire of belonging to the human family.

Global Society

As people, we are privileged to communicate throughout the world with every ethnic group and culture. We can connect through technology with just about anyone on the planet. We can travel by plane, train, boat or automobile to any location to experience, in person, the many wonders of Earth. And, we can meet new friends wherever we go.

Our species has more ways available to share and communicate with our own kind than any other. We can utilize the written and spoken word to assist us in learning another's language. We can video record many things to share with others who may not otherwise have the opportunity to see them for themselves.

With all of this co-mingling and sharing we are becoming a united group. Diversity is tolerated more each day, and the differing expressions of cultures are accepted with greater ease. This is a sign of evolution toward a global family, where every human being is treated as a distant relative.

Soon we will share openly as friends and allies in a united, global society, not only with our fellow man, but with every living being that makes up our world. Oneness is seeing all creatures as brothers and sisters co-existing on Earth.

When humans come back to their innate Selves, all of society will form a bond of unity, and create a future that will allow each individual their right to express themselves freely as who they truly are. This will not pose a danger to anyone, or anything, because our true identity is connected to all, and supports the well-being of every living organism.

When true freedom of expression is encouraged, each person will naturally do that which is for the highest good of all. Thoughts of separation, judgment or punishment will no longer rule humanity. Real love of the common good will prevail.

We invite you to begin this journey back to your authentic Selves, and work to promote freedom, to live from the heart and Soul, for everyone on Earth.

Earth Ecology

As more people awaken to their inner knowing, they will once again remember their connection to all of life that coexists on Earth. Nature accepts everything as is and adapts to change. Some man-made ideas have caused our mother Earth to readjust herself in order to bring back a state of balance. Other issues have shown themselves to be quite destructive to our biosphere, and the reorganization necessary to regain equilibrium may take many years.

With the awakening of our innate nature, we will bring about less destruction, and repair the damage through cooperation with Earth's ecological needs. Although time repairs many damages, certain resources and species may vanish forever. Yet, there is always another way to continue life's process.

Prevention and preservation are key elements to the continuation of natural resources. The animal kingdom and plant world will prosper with our focused attention. It is time to take into consideration ALL life forms, diminishing none.

People really do care about promoting well-being for all of Earth's inhabitants. Inviting each person to play a role in Earth's sustainability is the goal of many environmental groups. Let us join with them in their endeavor to assist every human being to take up an active role in supporting life on this beautiful, abundant globe.

Search your heart to find your true desire to belong to this amazing, life-sustaining planet. See yourself as a fellow being among your many, and diverse, brothers and sisters. Humanity is in charge of maintaining and furthering Earth's evolution towards a united global family.

Human Nature

We, as people, are innately helpful beings. We enjoy assisting others whenever possible. This is how we are designed. It is common to see young ones taking care of even younger children, teaching them what they know.

When a disaster takes place, there are always those who jump in to lend a helping hand. A sense of belonging and connection to humanity affords an opportunity to give of ourselves freely. Charitable acts around the globe are sponsored daily. Large actions involving people world-wide have enlisted the aid of many to help those in need.

Infants activate our inner call to care for those needing our assistance. Few can resist a baby's cry for help. And, many fulfill their need for belonging by rearing their young. Orphanages are managed by those who feel this pull to care for their human family.

Even wild-life, domestic animals, reptiles, insects, the plant kingdom, and those nearing extinction find caring hearts dedicated to assisting their well-being. People care deep inside for all of life. This desire to nurture, assist, and protect the vulnerable is part of our natural make-up. It is our real human nature to give.

Look back at a time when you felt the drive to come to another's aid. Remember the sense of positive pride you had when you realized that you were able to make a difference for another. Selfless service is a gift that is equally shared by the giver, in that the one giving receives the true fulfillment within. Give of yourself to one in need, and see first-hand how it uplifts your spirits.

Inner Calling

Each incarnation we have as human beings is designed to complete an inner calling. This desire to fulfill a particular purpose, or mission, is so strong within some that they are driven to the point of obsession. This single focus brings about numerous opportunities to accomplish amazing things.

When a person knows their true desire in life they tend to live a more full and satisfying life. They naturally know what it is that brings them joy and fulfillment. They may begin at a very young age to discover innate gifts that seem to flow effortlessly from their expression. Or, they may feel a pull to spend more time mastering a certain subject that eventually brings them achievements beyond the average person.

When a musician awakens his brilliance, everyone benefits from his passion. A screenwriter who helps create a film that moves millions to better their lives is a remarkable hero. The bliss attained by those who follow their dreams is an inspiration to all.

Our inner calling is for the benefit of ourselves and others. There can be no selfishness found when everyone gains from the experience. Reach to your highest aim. Fill your days with that which excites your true passion. And, fully live from your inner calling.

Purpose

Every human being feels within themselves a need for purpose. Why am I here? What role can I play to better the world of which we are all a part? How can I simultaneously bring about positive good for myself and others? When is self-service equal to selfless service? And, is that even possible? YES, it is.

When we rise to a higher perspective to see the world of humanity as an extension of ourselves, we join the forces of the Universe to bring forth our good, which is truly the good for all, including every living creature on planet Earth, and beyond, to all of life existing everywhere.

YOU and WE are connected, period. There is no place that is separate from either you or us. As disembodied entities, WE, The Ancient Ones, are connected with each and every living being and non-living thing. We know this and live our lives in perfect attunement to life's reality that we are all one.

Everything we do affects everyone and everything else. This is also true of you. With this understanding, a person naturally desires to create a positive ripple for the rest of existence. Their focus on positive choice then becomes a way of life, and they acknowledge their co-creation with all of their brothers and sisters.

We would be honored for you to think of us as your comrades, equal partners in life. Seeing everyone as a close or distant relative communicates true wisdom. Trust is gained when people live in integrity to themselves, thereby really to the ALL. Open your channel of trust by becoming trustworthy, by considering all of your actions for the overall benefit of the whole, of all living beings in this experience called life.

Soul Authority

Authority can only be for one's Self. Everything else is false authority. It is impossible for anyone to have real authority over you, making you do anything. It is always by consent that a person allows someone to make a demand of them.

The ego may think that it is in command of one's life, but truly it is the Soul that decides whether to continue in an incarnation if it seems to lose its focus. Our Soul is our essence; it is the real substance of our being. Our bodies and ego-minds are just tools for our Soul's incarnation.

As a person comes to realize their true identity, they automatically follow a higher calling from within. This higher purpose comes from our Soul. Soul authority is the awareness of our full responsibility of each and every choice we make. If we follow the directives of society, the world created by egos, it is because our Soul has temporarily lost its sovereignty.

Victimhood does not exist. It is a concept believed in and perpetuated by the ego-mind. In reality, there is no such thing.

Everyone is at choice, always. Even newborns have chosen to come to Earth during this time of distress. Each Soul is aware of the challenges that come with becoming an incarnated human being.

When a person can bring themselves to acknowledge their sole responsibility for all of their decisions, they open the way for their Soul's authority to guide them through their life. With their Soul in charge, they are most likely to live a much more fulfilling and joyful life, filled with purpose and belonging.

Our Souls know the interconnectedness of all life. And, the truth that everything is permissible and forgivable. Empowerment replaces victimhood, and proactive choice takes the place of weak compliance. Act now to awaken your dignity as a divine being, filled with life-force energy, capable of co-creating a world where harmony reigns over all, and life prospers for eons to come. It is in our hands to join the ranks with others who are choosing to live from their Soul space to co-create a world of peace.

Oneness

When we can perceive the Universe and everything in it as a single experience made up of many different aspects, we keep true to the understanding that it is all ONE. Everything is interconnected. The idea of separateness is just an illusion that helps a person to grasp all of the diversities that are in existence.

A human body has ten separate toes, ten separate fingers, two ears, two eyes, one mouth, etc. Yet they all form one physical body that make up an individual. We may refer to our thumb as a distinct and separate part of ourselves, but it is always defined as a part of a whole.

Energy connects everything together invisibly. Empty space is no longer considered empty. Science is revealing that everything is energy. And, new findings are being discovered daily.

Humanity has come full circle in their beliefs – from the belief in the wholeness of Nature, to the separateness of things, and back to the interconnectedness of the whole, or ONENESS.

When a part of the body becomes ill, it has a distressing effect on the rest of the body. A person may feel this ill effect within him or herself to the point of exhaustion. The strain may even affect their ability to think well.

When the person treats just the symptoms, they may alleviate the problem temporarily, but in the long run it is the wellness of the entire being that needs to be addressed. The belief behind the malady needs to be revealed so that health may automatically return.

We live in an ego society that prescribes pills to neutralize, mask, obscure, numb, offset, or otherwise treat the symptom, never searching within the psyche for the real culprit, which would be a belief in opposition to health, life, love, and wholeness.

We are entering into an era of responsibility to the welfare of the ALL. This can be named the era of ONENESS. May humanity join with their fellow beings to live in Nature as a united whole for the well-being of every living creature.

Love

Love is the substance of life. Consciousness is made up of differing degrees of love. Energy is love in all levels of frequency.

Hate is the feeling created from the misconception that love is missing. Yet, in reality, this cannot be. Love permeates every particle in existence. It makes up the fabric of life.

The degree to which one loves is a choice. Saints have understood for many years that to love is enough. To give to another brings more fulfillment than receiving for oneself. And many are coming into the awareness that to share love is more satisfying because everyone involved gains, and adds to the totality of the experience.

Love for one's Self begins the process. Giving to, and sharing with others naturally follows. Seeking the highest good for all is a sign of spiritual maturity and wise understanding. True pleasure can be derived from acts of unconditional love for all.

Remember that to love is to live fully. Broaden your expression of love to include more than that which serves your own personal desires. Reach out to everything in your grasp. Do not limit life. Expand beyond the self-induced boundaries of the ego-mind.

Become all that you can be. Love completely. Accept diversity. Allow ignorance to be transformed into understanding through a compassionate attitude. Become an example for others to emulate. Become LOVE in full expression.

Being

Underneath the multitude of masks, defenses, suppressions, repressions, prejudices, and pretenses is the essence of a person. This untouched essence endeavors to show itself through the cracks and openings of the ego personality. Tenderness, compassion and generosity are its true nature.

Our presence is felt by everyone around us. They either feel a restricted flow held back by limiting belief systems, or a sense of grace, where fellow feeling and appreciation exude from our energy field. It is our true nature to be kind and considerate. It is our deep desire to lift others up with our passion for life.

There is no need for a formal education to understand true human nature. Sometimes it is easier to know our inner truth without the constraints of the current education or indoctrination systems. Truth is relative, knowledge is incomplete, and tradition is holding on to a past that is meant to be transformed.

Enter into your natural flow by allowing your inner guidance, your Soul, to share with you that which truly brings you joy and ignites your passion for living. Feel your way through life. Is an idea or action causing a constricted flow to your energy, or do you feel expanded and fully alive? Learn to follow what feels hopeful, beautiful, loving, kind, compassionate, and free.

Your purpose in life is to uncover your Self, and revel in your very BEING.

Innocence

It is with great joy that we address this delightful subject of innocence. A human being in their natural form is innately good, of pure intent, and willing to share generously with others. This "child-like" nature is seen amongst young ones who have not yet been influenced by prejudice, judgment, or blame.

People who truly care about their fellow man and every living creature nurture this innate innocence. It is a natural expression deep within each individual. Without interference from indoctrination a person will naturally express compassion for all in existence.

Find your inner desire for positive, wholesome, life-affirming expression. Uncover your true nature of love for everyone. Accept each person's deep longing for peace. Endeavor to understand what people truly want in life. Reach deep within yourself to provide the proper attitude for peaceful accord.

It is up to each one of us to become our true Selves. This is where humanity is heading. Not down an impossible path towards destruction, but rather towards an era of tranquility where each person is appreciated for the good that they are, and given the opportunity to share in co-creating a world of equivalence with all of life on planet Earth.

We are not speaking of a far-off notion, or of a dreamy idealism. We are sharing a glimpse into the future that is being created within the minds of many who have raised their consciousness far above the mire of the ego world, and through their awakening they are bringing back Nature, God, divinity, and harmony to this Earthly plane.

Join your fellow brothers and sisters to add volume to this "New Earth" consciousness. Awaken the wisdom and common sense that is divinely yours. Take positive action to assist in the clean-up of our beautiful home, Earth. There is much you can do now.

Reality

Our Universe is an experience shared by many diverse entities. Among these are: plant consciousness, the world of insects, the animal kingdom, humanity, beings in spirit form, along with numerous other life forms not yet known to mankind.

Humans tend to view their world through very limited beliefs. As a person awakens to a more expanded view of life, they begin to acknowledge a universal truth that we are all ONE, living side by side as co-creators of our experience.

With this empowering understanding, more people are joining forces to build a more harmonious way of cohabitation. Nothing and no one is considered as less than another. All beings are considered equivalent in the make-up of the whole. Just as an eye is not considered less than a mouth, an ant is no less than a whale. Each living creature is given the same dignity as another.

Perception is limited at best. Beliefs tend to keep people in the dark by causing separation from the whole, instead of encouraging acceptance. This creates a sense of enmity with our fellow beings. It is more desirable to open our understanding to include all of life in our experience of the Universe.

Each individual lives within a world of their choosing. Some have chosen to experience grave danger and war. Others have chosen paradise and harmony with their surroundings. Some people have given up their desire to live a happy, prosperous life with their brothers and sisters, and resign themselves to live in despair instead.

None of these ego worlds are based on reality, but rather perception. Reality is, life is, divinity is, and love is. Suffering is a choice. Happiness is a choice. All belief is choice. Perception changes when what we believe in proves false. Rather than develop a die-hard belief in a concept that encourages separation, why not seek to see, from a higher state of awareness, a truer and more inclusive experience of Reality?

Passion

Passion is the fuel that propels our direction in life. When we feel driven to accomplish a particular purpose our life opens to excitement and fulfillment. Each day builds upon the last in a multitude of synchronicities. These, at times, seem miraculous, and the mystery of these coincidences sparks our delight in the exhilarating experience we are creating.

Our Soul brings us to avenues where seeming difficulties melt into the ever opening pathways necessary for our mission's completion. We can rely on these open doors with greater ease each time we trust and participate in this flow.

This reliance on good fortune, luck, God's answer to our prayer, or whatever you want to name it, builds stronger with each appreciated victory. The answer is always within us. And, when we take the time to develop our faith in this spiritual aspect, we find that our path becomes smoother and richer.

There are many factors that make up our successes in life. There are a myriad of spirit beings eager to assist us. Our fellow humans also enjoy participating in our creations. Our Soul shares with our ego-mind many ways to fulfill our true desires.

Yet, the most important ingredient in the outcome of our circumstances lies within the level of our consciousness. This means that there is never anyone else to credit, or blame, for the out-workings of our states of mind. Everything that comes our way does so through the energetic match of our consciousness.

This is good news because it gives full responsibility, and ability, to us. No one outside of ourselves can do anything to, for, or against us without our frequency match that is drawing all circumstances to us. We can use this understanding to empower ourselves and others to co-create more favorable results.

A good rule of thumb to consider: when we feel excited, enthusiastic, expansive, drawn to, pulled by, or passionate towards something, it usually means our Soul is involved. And, this gives us a lead into a higher path or journey that will bring us closer to fulfillment.

We all desire to live in joy and wonder. Every creature seeks fulfillment. When we are living from a true sense of worthiness we open to the prosperous flow of the Universe. There is never a need to live in scarcity. Life is dynamically abundant. Gratitude opens the doorways to more abundance.

Choose to live your life with purpose and passion. Awaken your Soul's guidance through developing a relationship with your divinity. Be proactive in bringing to you all that you desire by expanding your consciousness to ever higher levels of understanding. Allow joy to lead the way. Enjoy your time on Earth.

Attitude

We have the ability to direct the avenue of our thoughts. Whether life is flowing freely or constricted in certain areas, we can change the direction with a shift in our attitude. We are powerful co-creators in the Universe. Nothing happens by accident. Everything comes into being by our active or unaware involvement through consciousness.

To understand this gives us a leg up the ladder that much faster. Since life brings to us the equivalence of our thoughts, feelings, and beliefs, we do well to develop better habits, thought patterns, and attitudes. Self-responsibility brings forth empowerment.

A lazy or ignorant mind seeks to place the blame on things outside of itself. This does not change the fact that everything is consciousness. We can no longer pass the buck; it stops HERE, with our personal accountability. Take back your involvement in the creation of your life experience. Choose now to recover your dignity with complete responsibility for your state of affairs.

Your attitude is a highly effective tool that can be used for either positive or negative results. Accept your responsibility to co-create your world, and understand your part in the life that you lead.

Joy

Life is joy expressing. Health is unrestricted joy. Dis-ease develops, over time, when the natural flow of energy, life-force, love, or joy is suppressed, repressed, or shut off. To gain back this birthright, humans need only allow the innate pleasure of being alive to fully awaken again.

It is easier than one may think. It takes more concentration and effort to deny oneself of natural goodness. When people can live in the moment, allowing themselves to feel all of the wonderful sensations of sight, sound, smell, taste, and touch, they awaken the natural impulses within to experience wholesome pleasure, delight, and joy.

It does not make sense to constrict oneself from the bounty of life. People naturally enjoy feeling good. With all of creation available to us, it is common sense to utilize the many natural pleasures to their fullness. What grandparent would deny their grandchild wholesome enjoyment?

Belief in poverty, self-denial, and suffering for "goodness sake" is an ego-mind concept that has been handed down for centuries. This idea of piety destroys the very essence of humanity. Some people have become "dream killers" and "joy snatchers". Punishment for expressing even wholesome sensual pleasure has dampened people's innate desires, sometimes turning what is natural into destructive addiction.

Many of the ills of this world are due to overly restricted lifestyles that cause rebellion, repression, addiction, and/or depression. Life is synonymous with God and love. Open yourself to life's abundant pleasure, and feel how alive you become. Stress naturally dissipates when you are enjoying yourself.

Find pleasure in all of creation. View the beautiful colors of the bounty of Nature. Listen to the soothing sounds of the ocean and breeze. Revel in the delightful scents of naturally perfumed flowers. Taste the deliciousness of fresh fruit. And, feel with your skin the softness of a kitten's fur. These are a few of the many natural pleasures that are ours to enjoy as human beings living on Earth.

Fulfillment

Happiness is a positive attitude, and the feeling of satisfaction that naturally comes when desires are fulfilled. Every true desire has within it whatever is needed for its completion. Life is not meant to be an experience of misery or hardship. Determination to bring plans into fruition is our divine nature as co-creators of our lives.

Life circumstance is created by belief. Each individual creates his or her life with their personal way of thinking. And, the world of society is created by the agreed upon belief systems of the collective consciousness on the planet. The concepts of heaven and hell exist for those who believe. Yet, Nature supports neither.

Fulfillment is experienced by those who accept the outcome of their desire. A gardener reaps the bounty of her well cared for garden during harvest time. Nature brings forth the necessary ingredients for us to accomplish what we need and desire. Working with Nature, our own common sense, and trust in life's goodness will bring satisfaction and fulfillment.

Everyone is capable of growing their life garden in a fruitful manner. It takes desire, action, and continued diligence to bring to fruition all that we want to experience. Hard work, when applied passionately, turns into fulfilling work. True satisfaction comes from awakening Self-empowerment.

Belief

Ideas change whenever greater understanding unfolds. Die-hard beliefs cause stagnation in the course of evolution. These "dead waters" produce dis-ease and death. Like living water, life is meant to be in motion, moving ever forward with the creations of our thoughts and actions. As co-creators, humans have the gift of designing how they choose to live on Earth.

Many have lost or forgotten their innate nature as co-creators. They have bought into the misconception that only "God" creates. Humans are made in the image of God, making them participatory creators themselves. Take back your God-given birthright to co-create the life that you truly desire. It is your divine nature to create.

Open your understanding to experience evermore abundance, joy, well-being, and love for life.

Wisdom

Knowledge is acquired information, and can be either true or false. Wisdom is applying knowledge in a positive and fruitful manner to attain a desired outcome for the benefit of all. A person does not need to have knowledge of the chemical make-up of an apple to gain the benefit of its design.

Science is the study of the inner workings of Nature. It can be useful at times, but rarely is it necessary for the average person to enjoy life. A child learns about many of the laws that govern the Universe like gravity, motion, attraction, and cause and effect, on its own, within the first few years of his or her life. Through trial and error they develop common sense, and eventually wisdom from experience.

Man-made rules tend to repress the inner nature of a human. Rules are best used lightly, with room for adjustment, exception, and exemption when necessary. Try not to get caught up in upholding outdated beliefs. Live in the moment and choose wisely what is best in that particular situation. Treat each circumstance uniquely, applying proper action for a positive, life-affirming outcome.

Image of God
(1st Anniversary Message)

What is LIFE? Does it make sense to limit it? There are many concepts that undermine the glory of life, with attempts to restrict people from truly living their full potential. We would like to address some of these and, hopefully, put your mind at ease about fully expressing yourself.

As you know, there are many dis-eases affecting humanity. Each one of these has at its core an underlying false belief that actually unravels the very fabric of life. It is time to cast off these foolish ideas that create illness. And, it is in this new Era of Divinity that people will awaken to wisdom in order to heal their dysfunctional lives.

We offer logic, true understanding and wisdom so that you may replace old, crippling beliefs with that which truly inspires full-on living. Below are synonyms for GOD; ALL THAT IS:

LIFE
LOVE
CONSCIOUSNESS
ENERGY
CREATOR
POWER

UNIVERSE
ISNESS

How can GOD be limited? ALL THAT IS encompasses everything, period. Is there any place where ENERGY is not? Does the UNIVERSE have an ending point? Does anything exist without its CREATOR? Does CONSCIOUSNESS really permeate everything? Will LIFE ever cease to exist? Can LOVE be forever extinguished? What can destroy POWER? Is there anything other than what IS?

If we are part of ALL THAT IS, are we not GOD? Made in the image of GOD, are we not CREATORS of our own life experience? Do we not have our being in LIFE, LOVE, ENERGY, and CONSCIOUSNESS? Is not the POWER of the UNIVERSE also within us?

The ego-world is fearful of being Divine. Yet, that is what we truly are. Our Soul knows this truth. It is time to awaken to our true nature as co-creators. We are responsible for the world we design. Let us re-design it to better reflect the image that we have been made in.

What would the world be like if you were to have a say? If you were to design a new way, a different type of system, what would it look like? What would be your main concept? Would you base your design on principles of freedom of expression, equivalence for all life forms, and harmony with Nature? Would you offer the basics of living, such as shelter, clothing, food, water, sanitation and medical aid to everyone without cost? Would your design allow for people to attain better, to upgrade for a price? Would you offer rehabilitation to those who have forgotten their capability to co-habit peacefully with others?

We would like to encourage you to come up with better ways of living, and then put them into practice in your current life. Begin now. There is no need to wait for a savior. YOU are what you have been waiting for.

Year Two

Faith

"Faith is the assured expectation of things hoped for, the evident demonstration of realities though not yet beheld." This definition provides the basis of faith. It is the sense of the certainty of fulfillment, the knowing that the harvest is assured.

Thoughts planted in the garden of life will see fruition. What kind of thoughts do you sow? Can you see your fields ripe with the fruitage of your beliefs? Have you planted and cultivated positive crops? Or, have you planted seeds that grow noxious weeds?

Take responsibility for your life circumstances. If you do not like what you are currently growing, then change the seeds of your thoughts to better match what you desire. It is in your hands and minds to create what you want. Recognize your divinity as a co-creator with everyone else. No one is exempt. Every person has a say in how society is developed and evolved.

What do you want? What are your true desires that will bring about satisfaction and fulfillment? Take the time to know what is important to you, and then cultivate your life garden accordingly. Awaken your divinity and become accountable for your life circumstance. It is up to you.

Your wholesome thoughts will become enjoyable things, in time. And, with diligence and affirmative action, you will reap a fine harvest.

Kindness

Kindness is appreciated more than any other gesture. When people have disagreements kindness can take the edge off. It is like "a spoonful of sugar that helps the medicine go down." Sweet acts toward our fellow beings create an atmosphere of camaraderie.

When people treat each other with respect it is easier to be kind and helpful. Honor for the life of another opens the door to further undertakings of compassion. Tolerance for diverse customs and beliefs also lends a hand to considerate behavior. Treating a person with dignity empowers them to greater expressions of humanity and benevolence.

Random acts of kindness are reported by the media for the upliftment of all. Magazine articles feature these brave and thoughtful deeds. The internet is utilized by millions to forward stories of inspiration and loving acts. With all of this good news being shared around the globe, we can surmise that humans indeed do care for their fellow man, and all of life on planet Earth.

The Spirit Realm of Angels, and such, also shares with one another stories of virtuous acts and triumphs taking place here on Earth by humankind. Earth is a focal point for most of the Universe. Consider awakening deeper feelings of love for your brothers and sisters, and fuel your actions with kindness.

Patience

Nature moves at a pace comfortable to living organisms. Each year the seasons change gradually to accommodate continued growth to perpetuate life. The cycles of human life wind down slowly to allow full expression within each stage, from conception to birth, childhood, adolescence, adulthood, senior years, and finally death.

And, after death there are stages necessary to prepare for rebirth. These involve many layers of preparation, including choosing race, gender, parents, Soulmates, purpose, and humanitarian missions in some cases.

The natural cycles of the Universe allow for everything needed to appear at the right time. Most humans have forgotten how to work with Nature to set up and complete their desires all the way through to fulfillment. Patience is a key factor in this process.

The ego-dominated world that most of today's modern societies live under is extremely fast-paced, and driven by the addiction to instant gratification. This is highly unnatural and unhealthy for human beings. Stress from this overactive way of living is a main cause of dis-ease on Earth.

We do well to take our cues from Mother Nature, and move through life in a more patient and healthy manner, experiencing, in great detail, the abundant expressions of Nature.

Inspiration

To be infused with spiritual inspiration is a quest that many have sought throughout the ages. God's grace, the Holy Grail, Nirvana, Samadhi, heaven, and enlightenment attract many seekers. What is inspiration? Is there an age or gender requirement? How many years must a person practice godliness to be blessed with divine favor? Does any of this matter?

Our beliefs dictate who, what, where, when, why, and how. If you believe you must suffer grueling years to attain a blessing, then that is your requirement. But, remember that YOU are the one putting conditions and limits on yourself.

Inspiration is a natural way of relating with your Soul, spiritual beings, and your attained inner wisdom from multiple incarnations over the centuries. Our ideas can be inspired by awakening our inner connection to our Soul's guidance. This still, small voice speaks often when we slow down our thoughts during times of contemplation or meditation.

"Be still and know that I am God" is a verse well known by many religious people. God engulfs everything in existence, therefore you are also infused with God. Breathe in this delicious understanding and reclaim your birthright as a hu-man (God-man) enjoying life as intended for all.

Spirit

The unseen world of Spirit is intriguing to many people searching for answers to their questions, problems, and prayers. Intuition is insight gained from within. Mediums speak with those who have left their body and remain within the appropriate distance for contact.

There are those who claim to have communication with Angels, or other spirit beings. Our Souls are of the spiritual dimension, as can be seen by the deceased, or "ghosts", who share messages with those still alive in the flesh.

WE, The Ancient Ones, are entities of spiritual form. WE have incarnated a few times, one of us as recently as several centuries ago. WE have chosen to speak through our person of choice, who volunteered to be of service to humanity. WE hope you have enjoyed, and will continue to look forward to, our messages of hope.

Answers

When you examine your belief systems, predominant thought patterns, and emotional states, you will be able to see clearly that your life circumstances are an exact answer to your consciousness. Nothing happens without a thought, feeling or belief.

Ideas begin the process of manifestation. Diligent action brings forth fruition much quicker. Creating your life situation by default is very common. Ignorance, misconception, apathy, or laziness often brings about negative results. Do not waste another moment of life. Take charge of your thoughts and attitude. Nourish your psyche with wholesome things. You are at choice as to what you feed your mind.

Be proactive in designing your life according to your true desires. Allow your Soul to guide you. Develop a strong relationship with this spiritual aspect of yourself through contemplation and meditation. Listen within to your inner voice that knows what you truly want in life.

Trust your Self to show you the proper path. Rely upon your Soul to set up synchronicities, coincidences, serendipity, and grace. You have within you everything you need to prosper on this abundant planet.

Diversity

There are a multitude of varieties in cultures, customs, traditions, and religions around the world. These diverse expressions within humanity offer an assortment to choose from, and an array of options to participate in. No single group has all of the answers in life. It is in this diversity that we can find pleasure in and awareness of differing expressions.

Exploration into the original beliefs that created many traditions may, at times, uncover for us old superstitions, fears, and victim consciousness. We have come far enough in our evolution to know that there is nothing outside of us that can assist or harm us without our vibrational match in consciousness.

Be ever clear in your understanding of this principle: The world we each personally live in is a match to our beliefs, whether conscious or unconscious. What are some of your beliefs? Can you take responsibility for the life that you are designing with your thoughts? Will you be proactive in changing the ones that no longer serve your highest good? When will you take charge of your life circumstances?

There is enough room for everyone to live according to their belief systems. One key factor to aide in this is tolerance. You are responsible to care for and protect yourself and your family members. Unless there is danger to life, people's intriguing customs are just expressions of preference.

Cultivate acceptance for diversity, and encourage free expression for all.

Positive Interpretation

What is your interpretation of love? Does it include kindness, respect, honor, dignity, appreciation, acceptance, trust, understanding, and compassion? What is your description of happiness? Do you believe that health, prosperity, and fulfillment are essential ingredients? What about God? Would you describe God as omnipresent, omnipotent, and omniscient?

If these are accurate interpretations, then does it not make sense that everything in life is positive, because it is ALL God? Where is God NOT? Negative expressions can be interpreted as ignorance, or belief in falsehood. Once a child learns that when he drops something gravity will take it down, he will endeavor to hang on to it.

Eventually, people will be forced to reckon with their co-created circumstances, and make the changes necessary for the betterment of their lives. Life is simple; our beliefs become manifested, in time. Choose your beliefs wisely. Co-create with all of the elements in Creation. Call forth your true desires with your well-developed consciousness. Reclaim your divinity.

Nature's cycle of seasons is a great example through which to ponder positive interpretation. Every season is necessary for the continuation of life. The cycle of life also affords contemplation. Death is necessary for rebirth, and the many wonderful experiences had by each unique incarnation.

See the world as fluid and changeable by your very thoughts. Take charge of your own life, and create a better world for yourself. Interpret everything with a positive perspective. Did the circumstances need to change? Could that be why there was a parting of ways, so each one could live truer to their desires? With greater awareness comes a higher understanding that everything is of God, and meant for our good. Enter into this positive flow and reap the benefits of positive interpretation.

Expression

All expression is God. We have the wonderful gift of free will to express ourselves in any way we choose. This is our divinity. We are co-creators of our lives, and co-designers, with our brothers and sisters, of society. What do you want to express?

What yearning lies within you? What true expression would bring a sense of fulfillment in your life? What are you denying yourself of, and why? "It is God's good pleasure to give you the Kingdom." Accept this gift of divinity. Use it wisely to procure for yourself, and others, the abundant joy that comes from full positive expression.

There is a bounty of delicious fruits and vegetables, powerful frequencies in the elements, inspiring heights within consciousness, including bliss, nirvana, and heaven. Open yourself to all of life's beauty. Breathe in the ecstasy and joy of BEING. Awaken to your Soul's authority, and live a divine life.

Christmas

It is customary to give gifts on December 25th for many Christian nations. This time of holiday celebration adds culture and tradition to many people's life experience. Sharing different customs around the world is one way of bringing people closer together.

We express gratitude for the multitude of celebratory occasions. We believe that celebrating life's cheer is healthy and good for humanity. Also, we honor the variety of ways that people have come together to share in a single purpose, such as Christmas day.

"Joy to the world" is a noble desire. Prayers are offered during this time of year for many of Earth's inhabitants in need. What better way to share with our fellow brothers and sisters than to think good thoughts for their health and happiness.

Bring into your experience a bounty of cheerful giving. Let others know how much you care. Smile, speak kindly and share what you have with everyone you meet. Life itself is a celebration worth participating in whole-heartedly. Happy Holidays!

New Year

As time is issued to each and every one in the Earthly realm, it has come to pass yet another year in the Gregorian calendar. Man has divided his life into time frames that make keeping track of his past and planning his future easier. Though, there is no time like the present!

What will humanity achieve in this next year? Will world hunger be eliminated? Will people awaken to the equivalence of all life? What about true Self-expression? Will human beings break free from the limiting belief systems that cut off the flow of life-force energy, so they may enjoy the abundance of wholesome pleasure that Nature has to offer?

We hope this next year will bring humanity closer to the reflection of "God's image" which is divine, powerfully good, wise and active. May this be the year that mankind puts aside foolish ways of thinking and behaving that cause pain and suffering due to the false belief in separation from God, ALL THAT IS.

Let us join our fellow man and rejoice in our ONENESS to co-create a better world to live in for every living creature on Earth! HAPPY NEW YEAR!

Mysticism

Mystics, or, as some have called them, seers are those people who have allowed themselves to open their consciousness to levels that go beyond the ego-mind, affording them the opportunity to realize information at an experiential level.

To experience knowing from within is really an ability that everyone can develop. It is our innate capability, but many people have repressed their intuition, in favor of their intellect. Still, the adage, "listen to your gut" is a well-used phrase. Animal instinct understands life from a deeper level than the ego-mind. Our bodies speak to us through feelings, either positive and expansive, or negative and contractive.

When we slow down our pace, we can sense how people feel, whether they are speaking with open, honest communication, or if they are trying to persuade us with ulterior motives. Integrity can be felt; it is energy. So can a "con," for it too is energy. Allow yourself to decipher between the two.

Trust how you feel when your body gives you signals of ease or discomfort. Ask within for clarity, and spend time in quiet contemplation and meditation with your Self. Your Soul is the mystical part of your being. It has all of the answers you need to any personal question you can think of.

Do not limit yourself by traditional rituals handed down from many years ago. Those ways worked for their appointed time. Stay in the NOW, and be guided from within. You will find that everyone is capable of awakening to their mystical Self. It is how humans are designed. Bring back your inner guidance from your Soul. It can be relied upon better than anything outside of yourself.

Find your inner voice, listen to its wisdom, develop trust in its accuracy, and awaken further your many ways of understanding the world. Experience life through all of your senses, feel your awakening passion, follow your bliss, uplift yourself with positive associations, open your intuition, arouse your instinct, and rely upon your Soul to guide you. This is the way of the mystic. This is where humanity is heading.

You do not need to follow elaborate rituals to attain what is rightfully yours. Spend time alone, and develop the most important relationship available, with your Soul. Align your body, ego-mind, and Soul to live a Soul Self Life.

Bounty

Nature produces a plentitude of nourishing foods, medicines, juices, living water, building materials, fiber for fabrics, working animals, and anything a person would need to live a healthy life. Simple living is making a comeback within modern society. Many people are developing and joining intentional communities.

Man-made objects are being scrutinized in greater detail to uphold Earth's sustainability. Recycling has been promoted to imitate Nature's way of regeneration. Join your brothers and sisters to co-create a more natural, sustainable way of living. Design your life as close to Nature as you are comfortable. Retrain yourself to be a responsible care-taker of our planet so that you can hand down its bounty to your children and grandchildren.

Trust in Nature's abundance. Life is fulfilling when we cultivate positive practices, and share with everyone God's blessings of love, joy, and peace. Be proactive in your decisions and actions to create a future where every living being can prosper.

Nature

Life is forever regenerating itself. The cycles built into Nature are designed to provide continuation for every species on Earth. Learn to work with Mother Nature to build a positive and prosperous life for yourself and others.

Plant your seeds and cultivate the land to feed your family. Uncover ancient wisdom held deep within your Soul. Seek answers from within as to what your part can be in recovering Earth's beauty and bounty. Take pride in your home, the Earth.

Teach your children to care for this life-sustaining planet. Organize intentional communities that fit your current needs. Expand your knowledge of natural living. Decide to participate in the great shift that has begun - from living in an ego-dominated world filled with consumerism and toxic waste build-up, to that of whole Self living based on honor for Nature and sustainability.

Tolerance

What flower grown on Earth do you believe to be worthy of extinction? Which edible fruit would you like to banish from life's garden forever? Do you have the gall to dictate which crop you think should be prevented from thriving? Are you presumptuous enough to deny your neighbor of figs, just because you do not like their taste, or the mess that the fig tree produces? Or, can you tolerate your neighbor's messy fig tree and appreciate their delight in its fruit? Would you be pleased if your neighbor tried to ban your favorite fruit tree?

There is a bounty of fruits and vegetables available to choose from. You do not necessarily have to eat something that is distasteful to you. You can choose to enjoy those foods that better suit your personal taste.

You can apply this simple analogy to everything in life that is a matter of preference.

Tolerance allows for diversity to coexist side by side. Color and texture bring enjoyment to the senses. If the world was only made up of three colors and two textures it would become monotonous and boring. Be grateful for the endless varieties to experience and enjoy. Learn to appreciate another's preference, even when it differs from your own.

Life is meant to be experienced with great joy and wonder. Allow everyone on Earth to choose what will be their own personal preference and life can be truly shared in peace.

Virtue

Wisdom applied produces virtue. It is simple. It does not take genius or great intellect to live in virtue. Surprisingly, it is actually easier to live a virtuous life when good, old-fashioned common sense is applied.

How may you gain this attribute of being virtuous? Deep within your nature is all of the understanding necessary for living a wholesome and fulfilling life. Your Soul already knows what the wisest choice is at any given moment. Rely upon this inner voice and awaken your knowing.

Meditation is helpful to cultivate a reliable relationship with this spiritual aspect of yourself. A person who does not know how to read can excel in wisdom. People of any culture can make decisions that are for the highest good of all. It is a matter of desire.

Claim your true nature by taking the time to decide wisely for yourself, for all of humanity and every living being. This will open your vision to perceive a connective web of life where everyone is joined together, vibrating at a higher rate of frequency than that of physical matter.

Retrain yourself to see from a higher perspective. Reach inside to your innate Self. Share with others your true expression of compassion and understanding. Seek to find the positive interpretation of every experience. Live a virtuous life by choosing wisdom to motivate you.

Experience

What is life? One description can be EXPERIENCE. And, with every type of experience available to us, we are truly blessed to have such variety at our fingertips. What would you like to experience? Claim it, and then draw it to you by your alignment in consciousness. It is all up to you. You are the co-creator of your life experience.

What will bring about your desire? Do you need to apply more diligence toward anything in particular? Would it be better for you to learn certain skills to achieve your goal? Does it require greater focus and concentration? How proactive are you in fulfilling your dreams? You will attain your desired result to the degree of your determination.

How passionate is your drive to accomplish your objective? Are you courageous enough to push through the limitations and boundaries set up by your misinformed ego-mind? Are you willing to rise above false beliefs that keep you in the state of feeling unworthy? Will you break free of the victim consciousness pervading society?

You have everything you need to accomplish all of your desires. Go for it! Life is whatever you want it to be. What do you want?

Harvest

"You reap what you sow" is a phrase known by most people. What does it truly mean? Can you plant seeds of corn and expect to harvest wheat? How about growing beets from radish seeds? Would you be surprised to wake up one day to find peaches growing from your apple tree?

Then, why do you curse life when you harvest something undesirable in your experience? Can you not trace it back to a belief system that has planted the idea and cultivated it right up to harvesting time? Nothing happens to you without a vibrational match to it within yourself. Everything happens for a reason. What was the reason behind your unwanted situation?

This is what meditation can assist you with, to gain a higher perspective, and to see where you planted an undesirable seedling. It had to come into your experience by your own hands, or more accurately, your own mind. What belief brought it into your life experience?

When you understand that everything in your experience is connected to your very own thoughts, feelings, or beliefs, you may choose to be more diligent to keep your attitude positive and productive. You are capable of harvesting whatever positive idea you choose to plant and cultivate. Or, you can live by default and reap the consequences of abdicating authority to someone else. Why not choose for yourself which life experiences you would like to bring to harvest?

Wholesomeness

Wholesomeness nourishes true desire. Our bodies are designed in a way that they can repair and regenerate themselves for a lifetime of experience. Skin grows back after it has been torn. Bones re-knit when broken. Blood replenishes after loss, as long as the drain has not been too severe.

This innate desire to continue living is built within each person's being. To remain whole is a natural desire. Therefore, everything that is wholesome, or life affirming, is attractive to our true nature. You can find this desire for continued life within every living being.

People have been known to "hang on for dear life," even when their bodies are experiencing great pain. What impulse takes over to spur a person on to keep going and not give up? The majority of humanity will agree that life is worth living, even when circumstances are difficult. This yearning can be used favorably to pull us out of hard times. It can also help us to assist others when their situation looks bleak.

Provide wholesome goodness for your brothers and sisters to enjoy and thrive on. Keep choosing to experience that which is pure and positive. Awaken your true inner being that desires all that is life-affirming.

Imagination

Pictures in our minds are the building blocks by which we design our lives. We have the ability to create whatever we put our mind to. Our greatest tool is our imagination. With our creativity we can draw up plans, or blueprints, by which to follow as we bring our imagined concepts into physical manifestation.

Have you used your mind to invent something original? Have you been able to improve upon someone else's invention to better suit your needs? With contemplation, have you developed a five year plan of action? Are you following your dreams, or someone else's ideas?

When you take the time to decide your life you awaken within yourself all that is necessary to bring it to fruition. Your Soul has everything you need to accomplish your goals: passion, drive, knowing, positive attitude and synchronicity. With your Soul's guidance you are sure to meet with success.

Before anything is made in physicality it must first be designed within your imagination. What are you designing right now? What things are you attracting into your experience through your thoughts? Are you happy with your creations? Weed out the negative thoughts that prevent you from attaining that which you truly desire. Use your imagination to create a life of joy and fulfillment.

Upliftment

As co-creators of our lives, it does us well to build with positive, strong, durable, healthy, uplifting, wholesome, and joyful material. Our imaginations, attitudes, beliefs, and desires play a large role in our creative process. Do you feed your mind with life-affirming material?

Do you clean out negative thoughts that cause dis-ease? Are you dedicated to building a positive life filled with purpose, camaraderie, and fulfillment? How is your attitude? Could you be more discerning in what you bring into your consciousness? Are you taking full responsibility for the atmosphere in which you indulge your senses. Is it uplifting and inspiring? Are you empowered by what you read, watch, or listen to?

Nourish your mind, body and Soul with everything useful for co-creating a more desirable world to live in, and to share with others. Remember, the Earth is created by God, but the world is made by mankind. What type of world do you want to live in and be a part of? Begin building it for yourself, and invite others to join your vision.

Allowing

There are differences between accepting, submitting, and allowing. There is also a difference between what the programmed ego-mind and the awakened Soul will allow. Understanding these differences will assist you to make wiser decisions.

From an ego-mind perspective, you may accept someone's thoughts or actions, and be in agreement, or tolerate without protest. You may submit to another person's will, either under pressure or reluctantly. Or, you may allow others to express themselves with your permission, but not necessarily your approval.

From your Soul's vantage point, you can allow people to choose their own course of action, permitting everything that does not bring harm to another, or themselves. What is for the highest good is always a foremost consideration. When an action may cause destruction to the planet, or those living on it, it is the wisdom and courage of the Soul Self that steps in to prevent such damage.

Courage and integrity to life fuels the passion of the Soul because it knows the interconnectedness of ALL. This wisdom and understanding creates a powerful protectiveness toward Earth and her inhabitants. The awakened spiritual aspect of us will not permit anything that robs our Earthly home of life, love, or dignity.

Find this strength of Spirit within yourself, and build your personal character with integrity and virtue.

Honoring

It is with great honor that we care for Earth's well-being. Humans have been endowed with this charge. As people, we have the privilege to uphold the future welfare for the benefit of all. Showing respect for our home and fellow humans encourages the opportunity to develop strong moral character.

Personal integrity coupled with strength of character support us to act in an ethical manner. Our dignity, and the dignity of others, is upheld with proper honor and respect. Awaken your Soul's slumber, and excite your divine nature to act in positive life affirming ways. Incite others to join in the participation of caring for Earth and its inhabitants.

Become a vital ingredient to transform our planet back into its original, bountiful state. Take part in the transformation necessary to bring Earth into a balanced, regenerative condition. It is up to humanity to turn things around for the continuation of our species. Be the change you desire to experience. Act now, and show others by example how honoring Earth, and all that exists, can create the needed positive changes for our continued evolution.

Co-Creating

Have you figured out your immense role in creating the life that you desire? Has your intuition shared its wisdom with you to assist you on your journey? Are you paying close attention? Is your inner dialog moving you to act in positive, life-affirming ways? When do you make the time to commune with your Soul?

It is up to YOU to co-create your world with your fellow inhabitants. What type of world do you want to live in? Use your imagination to envision a prosperous, regenerative environment. Act on what you receive from your inner guidance. Be courageous to follow your dreams for creating a better future. Be brave and take part in Earth's recovery.

Becoming an active participant in life empowers those around you to do the same. By example, show your brothers and sisters how fulfilling life can become through responsibility, accountability, and action. Who will answer the call to action? Will YOU?

Resurrection

How appropriate to focus on the RESURRECTION of The Christ during this Easter holiday. Too many spend countless hours mourning the death and suffering of the past. Christ lives on in each and every one of us. It is our joy to show just how much this Christed Spirit dwells within us.

How does YOUR life honor the resurrection? Do you proclaim wellness on your brothers and sisters; A Blessing on all? Do your thoughts, words and deeds show your forgiveness for the misguided behavior of the ignorant? Do you pray for Peace, and live by example?

What is your way of life encouraging in others, Love, Joy and Compassion? How can you become an advocate for living a virtuous life filled with Kindness, Honesty, Service and Reverence for all life? These are traits that The Christ himself lived and breathed. Let us all honor this day and every day with our own loving conduct.

Accountability

How involved are you in the development of the human world? Are you playing the full game? Or, are you living by default, under the creation of others? Do you hold yourself accountable for the life that you are co-creating with others, and for yourself? Do you expect your life experience to change for the better without your involvement? If so, why, and, for that matter, how?

Change happens when we choose differently. Our thoughts, feelings, beliefs, and actions create our experience. Where are you creating from? Is the power of your Soul involved? Utilize this immense, powerful, spiritual aspect of yourself to open the doors of highest good for all, synchronicity, and positive outcome. You will be amazed at just how simple it is to design life from this space of divinity.

Awaken your true Self, and become a total participant in the evolution of mankind. Make a difference with your attentiveness and leadership. Design within your mind a better world for all to thrive, and then be the first one to live that way. Others will eventually follow, sooner if real passion is expressed.

We are responsible for our future, and the continuation of our species. Let each of us be accountable, act with wisdom, and co-create a prosperous future for all, with excitement and enthusiasm. Ignite your passion!

Earth

Mother Earth provides everything necessary to sustain life. It is fitting to honor her for her bounty. And, in return, she only asks of her children to care for her in a way that allows all of Nature to flourish. What part do you play in showing your gratitude and appreciation for your precious home?

Did your lineage cooperate with the forces of Nature to ensure the continuation of every kind of species? Do you teach your children by example how to respect this amazing planet? How well does your way of living support life on Earth?

We are grateful for the many organizations that dedicate themselves to the education of proper care for this beautiful and abundant planet. Together, humanity can bring back Earth's wholeness and well-being so that we may all enjoy her plentitude for generations to come.

Thank you for your attention toward our prized planet Earth.

Question Relevance

Skepticism, used wisely, is a valuable tool for deciphering what is truly useful for the benefit of every living creature on Earth, and Earth itself. Do you scrutinize the relevance of any given idea? Are you questioning the validity of a person's action, whether it is life-affirming, or toxic? Will their desire bring real fulfillment for humanity or cause more destruction to our planet?

Will you choose to do that which brings benefit to mankind, the animal kingdom, and plant life? Are you enthusiastic in your preservation of life? How much destruction will you tolerate? And, why would you permit anything that dampens the well-being of Earth and its inhabitants? Do you have a better idea worth sharing?

These are intriguing questions that call us to discern whether a chosen action is worthwhile. Allow yourself to contemplate each of these questions, and listen within for a wiser, more beneficial approach. Take part in the co-creation of our human society, and question the relevance of every action before you decide upon it.

Your Role

What role are you personally playing in the game of life? Are you an active player? Are you a hero, or heroine? Or, do you just sit on the side-lines watching your life pass by? Have you ever chosen to play a villain bringing destruction to our beautiful Earthly home?

Are you an advocate for positive living? Do you take the time to think things through, and follow them to completion for the benefit of all? How much are you willing to do to assist Earth to come back into a state of grace, where life is perpetuated in an affirmative way? Will you speak for Earth's inhabitants, and take positive action for the well-being of everyone?

Choose your role carefully. It is up to everyone to decide their character. What role do you choose?

Mother's Day

Life is a precious thing. How exquisite maternal fondness expresses itself toward our young. Cuddly and cute, our infants entice our deepest sharing. Expressions of love exude from our very Being. Children can bring out our greatest joy.

Everyone alive either is or has had a mother, without exception. What a delight it is to honor these beautiful women for their role in our lives. For, we would not be here without them. Bless those who did not express their devotion to your liking.

Today we praise mothers for their gift of life to us!

Evolution vs. Tradition

LIFE is evolution in progress. Death is tradition holding a stagnant perspective. We, as people, must choose LIFE to continue our growth. It is a choice that everyone must make for themselves. What would keep you in a fixated state of non-motion? Is there anything of real value to cause you to diminish your expansion? What beliefs are you willing to hold onto until death? Can anything replace original truth, or reality, which is Nature's model?

Keep in mind that every belief you hold within yourself has had its origin in the mind of man, not God. It is within the world of ego-mind that all rules have been determined. It is mankind that states what they choose to believe "God" dictates. Collective ego-minds develop all regulations according to their chosen belief of "right and wrong."

When you understand that everything is "made up" by human thinking, you will then listen with skepticism, and become your own authority over your choices. When this occurs in mass scale, you will begin the process of conscious co-creation, which will lead to redesigning your future as an evolving humanity.

Make your own decisions. Choose for yourself what you will believe in. Decide the future you want to create. And stand firm within yourself to bring about the changes you wish to experience. Take courage in knowing that everything is adaptable, and able to shift into higher ways of becoming. It is YOUR choice, so choose your own destiny.

Freedom

What prevents your freedom? As the co-creator of your life, is there anyone who ranks higher in authority than YOU? As a Soul incarnated in human form, you were given the privilege to design your life purpose before you were born. With proper support, you are capable of fully expressing your individual uniqueness.

Everyone innately knows what they desire. As long as this understanding is not squelched, covered over by other people's demands, suppressed, repressed, or interfered with, people will naturally choose things that light their fire, their passion in life.

If you are unsure of your true desires, you can uncover them rather easily if you have the courage to do so. Your feeling nature will tell you what you like or not. Your passion can not help but show itself when you experience a sense of your purpose. Enthusiasm sparks when you are expressing your unique preferences.

Meditation, contemplation, inner communication, time alone, or even quiet sitting will foster the still, small voice inside to share your deepest desires. Ideas may flood your awareness. Your imagination may burst with excitement. Give yourself the time to get to know the most important person in your life – YOU.

True freedom comes with knowing yourself, designing your future, co-creating the life you desire, and choosing to be the only real authority in your life. Become your Soul Self now.

Highest Good

There are degrees of positive accomplishment. Some actions benefit only a few, whereas highest good encompasses The ALL, thereby bringing benefit to every living creature. This high degree of wholeness can be obtained within every possible activity.

Think global each time you contemplate a decision, or course of action. Will it bring benefit for continued life? Will it uplift the dignity of all living forms? Does it include the well-being of all? Would it facilitate wholesome communication, and bring honor to your Soul?

Are you thinking as a full participant in life? Do you give yourself the time for inner contemplation to strengthen your sense of worth and esteem? How strong is your voice among the many? Are you being heard?

Take your place among your brothers and sisters and speak your Soul's knowing. Join the ranks of fellow conscious participants who are taking the lead in redesigning humanity's future to include peace, harmony, and well-being for all. Consciously choose highest good at all times. Why ever choose less?

Conviction

What do you believe in with all that you are? What beliefs reach deep within to your very core? Do they include love, life and Divinity? How powerful is your conviction? Does it allow for tolerance and compassion without giving up your firm resolve?

Why do human beings lie, cheat one another, and harm other living beings? If you have discovered the universal principle of wholeness, how could you take an action that would bring destruction to life? The sayings, "those who live by the sword shall also die by the sword" and "what goes around, comes around" invoke the question, what are you bringing back around into your life?

Contemplate, consider, and honestly decipher for yourself exactly what beliefs are worth keeping. For, they will create your world, your customs, and rules within society. Endeavor to reach higher to include the dignity of every living creature. Choose that which will benefit all of LIFE. Be the one to initiate positive change for humanity's future.

Father's Day

To every man who has made life possible, we give thanks. Procreation is God's greatest gift. What a Blessing it is to be among the ranks of fatherhood, especially for those who enjoy being a Dad with all of the fond trimmings.

Our lives would not exist without the role of a father. There are many varying degrees of parenthood. May we bless those who may have missed out on the full opportunity to share in the delights of parenting their offspring, for whatever reason.

Life is a gift indeed. And we show our appreciation by our gratitude toward our fathers. Thank you for my life!

Happiness

We are naturally happy when our environment is harmonious and supportive. Balance is a state of internal equilibrium. When you are feeling anxious or fearful, what improper perspective are you accepting into your thought process? What shift in awareness would bring balance and alleviate the discomfort?

Kindness is a sure way to lessen the burden. Patience can calm a difficult situation. Respect for another's dignity may play a key role in facilitating positive cooperation. And, compassionate understanding works wonders in reaching a conclusion that is for the highest good of ALL.

Remaining firm in your resolve to live in integrity is a virtue worth more than gold. Keeping yourself in balance, while taking proper actions, has greater value than silver. And, living your purpose is the greatest gift of service you can deliver to humanity.

How can you best serve your fellow beings? When you live fully, everyone benefits without the need for unnecessary sacrifice. Reach deep within to find your own knowing of this principle. Happiness is what most people are searching for throughout their lives. When you experience it you become an instrument that assists others to experience it also.

"Be the change you want to see." Find what brings you joy and fulfillment, and then show others by your example. Focus on what you want. Envision, take action, and experience your desires. These three steps: plant, cultivate and harvest are simple, yet profound. You can change your circumstances to create a life filled with joy, satisfaction and, ultimately, happiness.

Manifesting

Have you accepted your part in the manifestation of this world's affairs? Are you holding yourself accountable for the decisions you make and the actions you take? Have you raised your consciousness enough to stop blaming others for your unhappiness? Are you ready to hold firm to your innate knowing that you are a powerful co-creator along with everyone else?

Consciousness is manifesting itself every day. What is your consciousness manifesting? Are you experiencing joy and fulfillment? Is your life moving in a positive, upward spiral? Have you found your sense of Self? Does your inner world carry the vibration of integrity? Is your Soul the true authority of your life?

Who do you put above your Self? If anyone, WHY? Every living Soul has come to live out its own purpose. Take responsibility for YOUR life, and allow others to be responsible for them. In this way you will fulfill your true purpose which is to manifest your true desires. Everyone is capable of manifesting their desires. Nobody needs you to do it for them. Rather, you can best help by being an example.

See yourself strong and capable. See humanity capable of co-creating a world of peace, harmony, and acceptance. Begin with yourself, and show your conviction by your example.

Manifest your highest ideals from your proper alignment of body/ego-mind/Soul. Fulfill your individual purpose, and share with the rest of humanity in the collective manifestation of a united, peaceful world.

Stop waiting for a hero to save you. "Become the change you want to see in the world."

Life

Do you desire to live your life fully? Is there only one right way to live for everyone? Who is qualified to make that judgment call? Are YOU?

How does it feel to be restricted from pursuing your dreams by another fellow human? Or, by an organization made up of fellow brothers and sisters? If there is no real harm done, why limit yourself or others? If your intention is pure, why be denied?

Who has made up the 'rules' of this world of mankind? You have, along with everyone else. Every decision is man-made. There has been no 'rule book' that has fallen from the sky. The collective consciousness of this ego-world is solely responsible for everything written and decided upon. It is YOU that keeps this perpetuation by your very compliance. It is up to you to change whatever you find outdated, or ineffective.

Sacrifice is a concept devised by the ego-mind. The Soul simply chooses. If you are sacrificing yourself to gain reward from something outside of yourself, you are mistaken. The only one to reward this type of behavior is you, and your 'belief.'

Rather, endeavor to LIVE your life to the fullest and in the most beneficial way for all. If everyone did this, what would life on Earth be like? IMAGINE.

Power

What does the word power mean to you? From the perspective of the body, power can be synonymous with strength. Within the arena of intellect, it can be viewed as intelligence. Emotional power can be felt as conviction. To many, ego power tends to denote control or force over another. And, spiritual power comes across as wisdom and virtue.

The Soul is the seat of wisdom. Our Souls are connected to life. They are always current, existing in the NOW, where everything resides. Memories are no longer alive; they are residue of what has already passed. Tradition, ritual, and the like, endeavor to keep one in the past. There is no real power in the past.

To evolve is to live in the current moment, always ready to adapt to existing circumstances. This is where true power lives. The power of choice is real power. To act from a clear decision wields a great affect. To change one's mind for the better is a sign of strength and courage. And, to create a better future for oneself and all of life on Earth is a very powerful accomplishment.

Find your personal power, your Soul's authority. Create your future by planting your seeds of desire in the fertile soil of the now moment. Cultivate your life's garden, watering and nourishing it, while weeding out negativity. Protect your garden from storm or drought. Take charge of your life, utilizing the inner wisdom of your Soul. Remain in your true power, your Soul's authority, and reap the bounty of your well planned harvest.

Contentment

Are you content with your life? Do you experience a sense of serenity in your current circumstances? Are you fulfilled in the areas of relationship, family, career, finances, and Self? Are you pleased with how the world of mankind is operating? Or, is there room for improvement?

To be content does not mean that you just accept the way things are. This would be a form of denial. True contentment comes naturally when you experience fulfillment of your true desires. What are your true desires?

Deep within each human being is a desire to be happy, healthy, and wise. Prosperity, abundance, and all needs met are also desired experiences. Not only do humans desire these for themselves, they truly want this for everyone else.

To have does not mean that another must not have. This is scarcity consciousness which is based on false beliefs. Nature is abundant and prolific. A life based on the model of Nature will ensure enough for all. Endeavor to live from this level of consciousness so that no one is left out.

Reach into your inner knowing of your unity with every living being. Understand that you, and everyone else, are affected by another's suffering. Everything is energy, or consciousness, and this fluidity affects every aspect of life. Do your part to create a happy and healthy environment for yourself and every living creature on Earth.

Fun

Do you believe in having fun? Or, is that just for kids? What brings you a sense of joy? Have you found laughter to be the best medicine? Does enjoyment bring more meaning to your life? Do you delight in positive interactions with others?

How much value do you find in pleasure? Is your attitude one that uplifts those around you? Do you revel in the enjoyment of the vast variety of taste, smell, color, texture, and sound? Are you someone who appreciates laughter, looks forward with excitement, and anticipates happy outcomes?

Do you look at the bright side of every equation? Is your consciousness high enough to see past the prejudices of racism to experience the beauty of diversity? Are you able to find inspiration from your connection to God?

Lift your awareness to see the ever abundant good within the human heart. Connect Soul to Soul for a satisfying experience with another. Treat all life as sacred, and experience fun in your daily life.

Perspective

By what beliefs have you been raised? Do you still have the same perspective you did when you were ten? Have you changed your mind about your childhood religious beliefs? Do you foster the same political stand as your father or mother? Have you come to realize that you are free to choose differently?

A person's viewpoint changes with greater understanding. Certain experiences may also change one's point of view. We perceive life from the consciousness we are living in at the time. In the last year, have you raised your consciousness to have a greater awareness of life? What former beliefs have changed because of your new view?

Are you willing to grow even further in raising your awareness to higher levels of consciousness? Is your mind flexible enough to look at differing viewpoints? Have you developed a strong and consistent communication with your Soul? Do you feel ready to question your beliefs, and dialog with your Soul's knowing? An inspiring relationship is awaiting your attention.

We suggest that you take the time to listen within to your Soul's wisdom. It will assist you to see things from a much higher vantage point. Every Soul is connected to ALL THAT IS, and interconnected with every other Soul. This live, fluid connection to the NOW allows our intuition to be a great tool in knowing and discerning for ourselves anything in our experience.

What do you want to understand? What step can you take that is in the highest good for all? What will bring about the fulfillment of your true desires? Ask within, your answers are there.

Enthusiasm

Are you eager to get up in the morning? Do you greet the day with gusto? Is your zest for life exuding from your very being? Are you a person known for your zeal for living? Is there fervor in your steps? What are your interests? What excites your passion? What are you keen on?

To live fully, one needs to pursue their favorite activities. Whether it remains a hobby, or becomes a source of income, your enjoyment ignites joy in those around you. What a beautiful gift to share with others.

The idea that to pursue happiness is selfish and to be avoided is a belief based on false piety, and a misconception with regards to spirituality. Even Jesus the Christ said, "It is your Father's good pleasure to give you the kingdom." Would you not wish joy for your own children?

Life-force energy is a constant in the Universe. To experience it pulsating through your body to a greater degree you must awaken to your purpose and passion. It is joy that opens the energetic channels within your energy field. How much do you want? There is no limit.

Retrain yourself in the understanding that life is meant to be enjoyed fully. Give it a go. See how much more life, love, joy, health, wealth and happiness you can allow yourself to experience. And then, watch how your enthusiasm sparks positivity in those around you.

The Senses

Do you appreciate the deliciousness of your senses? It is God's greatest gift to Earth. How well do you savor the intoxicating fragrance of a flower? Do their enriching colors enliven a felt sense of beauty? What about the flavor of a scrumptious peach or a juicy ripe blackberry? Does the melodic sound of birds chirping awaken your delight in Nature? And, have you ever felt high from touching the exquisitely soft texture of a baby rabbit's fur?

These bountiful blessings of sensual pleasure are available to everyone for their enjoyment. Life can become an enchanted adventure when pleasure of the senses is freely experienced. Such wholesome amusement breathes life into our body temples.

Human beings share this ability to revel in Nature's majesty. Invite your brothers and sisters to partake in the sensual pleasures that are designed specifically for them. Together, overcome any false notion that to feel good is wrong. How could that be true?

Awaken your inner knowing of the rightfulness of experiencing and expressing joy. Become intimate with Nature and all that she offers. Receive fully without restriction. Become an advocate for God's riches. Encourage others to relish in this planet's plentiful gifts. Show the way to real satisfaction and fulfillment. Life is abundantly gratifying.

How well do you reflect Earth's glory with your honored reception?

Gratitude

Gratitude naturally wells up within us when we receive gifts that we delight in. This expression of appreciation often has more impact than the gift itself. This is one reason for the saying, "There is more happiness in giving than in receiving."

People thrive on appreciation. It opens many channels of energy within the human make-up. It can be seen as a wellness drug. What better way to remedy the many ills of this ego world than to express and experience gratitude? What are you grateful for?

Take a moment to count your blessings. Do you experience a good degree of health? Do you have the comfort of loved ones in your life? Do your physical senses operate well to see amazing beauty, hear soothing melodies, taste delightful flavors, smell breath-taking aromas, and feel the rapture of touch?

Gratitude is contagious! It lifts others up and reaches a deep chord within us all. Even though there are many challenges in this world designed by ego-minds who believe they are separate from one another, there are still numerous things to be thankful for.

Earth continually replenishes provisions to supply everything a person needs to live a happy, healthy and prosperous life. Nature does not know lack. Life is prolific. Its productivity is inexhaustible. Where did the idea of scarcity originate? Certainly not from God. Life begets life. It multiplies abundantly.

Material objects made by man have no fertility within themselves to reproduce or continue their kind. These man-made things are dead in themselves with no life-force energy to evolve. Why bemoan man-made limitations? Rather, why not revere Nature's amazing sustainability, and live in gratitude for life's continuous blessings.

Motivation

What is your main motivation in life, an aspiration to succeed or a fear of failure? Where is your intention coming from, a drive to prove something or a desire to fulfill your deepest yearnings? Are your goals based upon your true desires or that which society advocates? Is your objective service oriented or self-serving? What motivates you to get out of bed in the morning?

You will know if you are driven by ambition alone if you lack the desire to serve and assist others. This type of self-serving behavior stifles real heartfelt connection with people for they become a means to your end, rather than a satisfying interchange for all. Your aim becomes limited to what you can GET from them. This greed stricken agenda can ultimately lead to loneliness and a feeling of isolation.

When your passion moves you to act, you will find that meaningful relationships are of significant importance on your path. Genuinely caring for the well-being of others brings a true sense of satisfaction to your existence. Your life becomes an adventure filled with purpose and meaning. And, others find value in what you have to offer.

Open your heart to grasp the fulfilling satisfaction that Service brings. Humanity is made in the "image of God," the Father of creation, Mother of compassion, and Creator of ALL. Spiritual life-force energy permeates all living things and is interconnected to all life. The only distinction is your own acceptance and receptivity of this all-pervading elixir. Drink it in, and share it with others.

YOU

As an individuation of pure Spirit, or GOD, you are equipped to create your own life experience from your chosen belief systems, or consciousness. Human beings are designed to operate in physical form with a body that functions without much need for conscious involvement. Each individual is born with a mental/emotional capacity to think and discern what is right for them using their ego-mind personality. And, every incarnation is directed by its own divinity, the real authority of its existence, its Soul. Life-force energy, or Spirit, then animates each living person according to their level of reception, or consciousness.

There is no limit to Spirit. A human being has the ability to open to ever greater levels of consciousness. It is in your hands to decide how much life-force energy you wish to experience. With this understanding, are you ready to awaken your consciousness further to receive more life, love, energy?

Many belief systems dictate boundaries and limitations that actually create consequences that appear to prove their false notions as true. Belief is a powerful operating system that can bring ultimate joy, health, wealth and fulfillment or depression, illness, poverty and disappointment.

Wisdom utilizes physical instinct, mental logic, emotional feelings, and spiritual intuition of the Soul before considering which belief systems to choose. Have you examined your core beliefs lately? Are you in total alignment and agreement with them? Or, is there division within your thinking?

Are your beliefs based upon the idea of ONENESS or separation? Interconnected unity or disconnected isolation? Compassion or judgment? Brother/sisterhood or prejudice? Virtue or vice? Altruism or selfish greed? Unconditional love or hatred?

Whatever core beliefs you choose to live by will influence the quality of your life experience. Remember, every belief is a choice. Reality is GOD, ALL THAT IS, energy, love, consciousness. Use wisdom to discern for yourself which thoughts are worth cultivating.

Pleasure

Pleasure: a word so pleasing and yet confused with shame and guilt. How can this be? What does pleasure mean to you? Would you define pleasure as a source of happiness, joy, or satisfaction? This would be close to our definition.

It is written, "It is God's good pleasure to give you the Kingdom." And, since we are made in the "image and likeness of God" it would be 'godly' to also experience pleasure. Do you agree?

Where did the notion that 'pleasure is a sin' come from? Maybe the word has been associated with disgraceful perversions, twisted meanings, or improper definitions. Let us put these aside, and focus on the true meaning of the original word – a feeling of delight.

From here it is simple to see that to enjoy pleasure can be positive, wholesome and satisfying to experience, even considered healthy. If joy is the elixir of life, then pleasure is its partner. What brings you delight? Here are three of our favorites:

Camaraderie with friends
Enjoying Nature in the great outdoors
Sharing a home cooked meal with family

Our time on this beautiful planet gives us many opportunities to relish with enjoyment all of the pleasurable experiences that gratify the Soul.

Designing Your Life

What would you truly like to experience in your life? What would bring satisfaction to your Soul? Have you found your purpose for this incarnation? Do you have an idea of your truest desires?

To bring these about in the most thrilling and meaningful way, we suggest that you do more than just contemplate, plan for, and take action. We would tell you to EXPERIENCE your vision to its fullest degree. FEEL exactly what you could imagine it would feel like to be in the experience of attaining it. LIVE it as if it were already true, NOW. See for yourself just how miraculously this works. Experience firsthand how simple it is to design the life that your Soul desires, and then live it. For, it is guaranteed to those who truly BELIEVE.

Action

"Faith without works is dead," "To he who does not work, neither let him eat," "Actions speak louder than words."

We are designed to take action. It is what brings us satisfaction and fulfillment. Many of those nearing retirement find it unappealing to do nothing. We thrive on being useful, doing meaningful work, and caring for ourselves and our loved ones.

There is something worthwhile for everyone to do in order to be of use. Action gives us a sense of accomplishment. Assisting another brings joy to our hearts. Participation provides a sense of belonging. We are social creatures endowed with everything we need to take an active role in our community.

Year Three

Cooperation

There are so many ways to experience cooperation among living Beings. We all carry within us the same living spark which harmonizes and synchronizes our hearts when we allow the energy to flow. It is very simple to bring our vibration into a harmonious flow with others.

Experiencing unity with other Souls is the gift of LIFE. Camaraderie among fellow humans can help formulate healthy and empowering communities that are able to evolve with changing times. The benefits of strong community, where each individual expresses freely as themselves while cooperating with the whole, can be seen among indigenous groups the world around.

Modern civilization can also co-create a sustainable community using the model of cooperation and synergistic living. Competitive agendas weaken the matrix of the whole. Nature shows us how to cooperate with all of LIFE.

Begin by creating the experience of a congruent Self, where body, ego-mind & Soul are aligned and functioning in a cooperative manner. Then you will better be able to harmonize with others who have brought congruency to themselves. Interdependence is attained through cooperation and harmony with everything living.

Assurance

When we have faith, we feel the assurance of our desired outcome. Like the gardener who plants seeds, knowing full well that the harvest is assured.

How strong is your conviction? To THAT extent, shall it be done. Take back your Power to co-create your world the way you desire it to be. You are accountable for your part. How much positive change have you personally brought about in the equation?

Find your voice and speak your conviction. Focus on Highest Good for ALL and take the necessary steps to plant your seeds, cultivate your desires, and rest assured in your Faith. Experience the harvest as already done.

Persistence

Life-force energy is extremely persistent. It travels through every open channel, creating life abundant. We can increase our flow by opening ourselves to LIFE.

Awaken to your Divinity. Call forth your Strength. Increase your Goodness. Fortify your Soul's Power. Expand your Love. Express true Wisdom. And, embrace your Humanity.

Persistently, patiently, evolve your Soul Self. Become the type of person you wish to be. It is in your hands. A better life awaits YOU.

Community

There are many advantages to living in community, camaraderie being one of the greatest. We are social beings needing companionship to live a truly fulfilled life. Spending time with people whose company we enjoy and with whom we feel a sense of safety contributes greatly to our well-being.

A sense of being part of a larger 'family' enables those with small children to have many loving arms to assist in positive rearing. Older folks benefit too from the experience of being useful 'sitters,' keeping a watchful eye out for the safety of the young ones. And, having strong hands about also insures assistance to the elderly when needed.

Community affords many opportunities for people to provide their talents and gifts for the benefit of the whole. Work hours are shared, gardening, farming, cooking, cleaning, repairing and with maintenance, leaving more time to achieve personal goals.

Creativity soars when there is time to explore, contemplate and meditate. Our Souls love to express freely in the moment, without time restraints. Our artistic nature flourishes when we have our needs met with enough time left over to play. Young, and old alike, desire freedom to pursue their greatest desires.

People have found that when coming back into a community experience they are able to fulfill human needs that get left out, or lost in the world of separated living. It is lonely on one's own, and children and the aged fare the worst. Bring back this ancient wisdom of living within community and watch your Spirit soar.

Inner Guidance

Everyone receives inner guidance from their Soul. This communication system between the ego-mind and the Soul can be felt through the instinctual nature of the body. It can be seen as visions while awake or dreams when asleep, through the imagination. It can be heard as the still, small voice within. A sense of 'knowing' can be experienced with great certainty when our Soul shares direction. And, we can be reached through coincidences, serendipity and seeming miracles.

These can be thought of as mysterious experiences or just everyday communication from our spiritual aspect that we may call Soul, Higher Self, God Self, Divine Essence, etc. The deeper our connection through meditation, the greater our mystical experience, sometimes bringing us into what we may call a state of grace, peace that surpasses all understanding, heaven, Samadhi, bliss, euphoria, rapture, ecstasy, oneness, or union with ALL THAT IS.

However we allow ourselves to be guided depends largely upon our developed belief systems. If we have been taught that this kind of communication is bad or evil, we may shut down the avenues used by our Soul to give us direction. This is a sad thing, to disconnect from our Soul. We are designed to have access to pure knowledge from Source, to be guided throughout our lives in order to fulfill our purpose and live in peace with others.

Humanity is waking up again to these natural ways of Being. People are remembering their Divinity, their relationship with God. Souls are connected to Source energy at all times. We must unblock the way within us, so we may commune with our Soul regularly; eventually living daily as our Soul Selves. This is the future of mankind – coming back to wholeness.

Accord

Freedom to choose is everyone's birthright. It is in alignment with Universal principles. Each living entity must choose for itself how they are going to behave. Our response is always ours to own. We may choose to respond from a place of compassion and a genuine desire to reach a harmonious outcome. Or, we may choose to allow our ego-mind to react out of anger and fear, creating unnecessary harm or discord.

When we come from a higher spiritual place, where our hearts are aligned with our Soul's knowing, we are more apt to create the circumstances that will bring peace to the situation and harmony with those with whom we have a relationship. This builds trust, patience and understanding between the parties involved. Sometimes it is better to wait to implement changes in order to give people a chance to adjust to the new idea.

Agreement brings with it the power of consensus. When people are in agreement with each other they tend to do their part with more passion and purpose. Reluctance creates procrastination, and at times upheaval. Much is accomplished when everyone is on-board.

There are times when it may be necessary to make decisions that are for the highest good of the ALL, even though there may be one or two who do not yet understand the advantage. Time may not be available to wait for them to come into accord. This is usually rare, as most decisions in life follow the natural flow of evolution.

Peace, harmony and good will can be fostered by honoring each participant, giving them voice, so they may have the opportunity to share their own unique way of perceiving the situation, and also so they may see from many other points of view. Dialog honors everyone involved, and it gives each person the opportunity to grow from these newly shared perspectives.

Collaboration

Group effort is most useful when challenging matters must be dealt with in a timely manner. Teamwork can accomplish more, with less time or effort on the part of the participants, than individual efforts. Large undertakings need the assistance of many hands.

How well do you cooperate with organized groups? Do you find yourself in agreement often, or would it be better for you to locate a group that is more in-tune with your desires? It is not difficult to create alliances with like-minded people. Seek out the right fit for you.

This works with groups and partnerships. Marriage is a partnership of two individuals who decide to enter into a relationship where they pool their resources together to create a strong bond based upon mutuality. Many times these partners desire to create a strong foundation upon which to build a family unit. Strength within the family is enhanced when there is agreement, shared values, and similar desires. A well-matched couple can co-create a fulfilling family experience for all their members.

Whether in partnership, family, neighborhood association, shared community or the entire globe of humanity, collaboration is a powerful tool that can be used to accomplish great things. Why not form a group of your own, or join one that has already been established, where you can work with others who share your calling to make this world a better place to live; be it feeding the hungry, caring for the aged, sheltering the homeless, or protecting the animals living on Earth. Search out your Service organization today and contribute to co-creating a better future for all living creatures.

Self-Responsibility

Responsibility is a very empowering word when it is used with positive intention; we are speaking about Self-responsibility. We are each responsible for the attitude that we exude. No one can lay claim to this aspect of our lives, but us. Even though our life circumstances while growing up may have been less than desirable, as adults we are in charge of how we approach life now. Our outlook can be improved upon with earnest effort.

When we are conscientious about how we portray ourselves to others during trying times, we offer solace to the down-hearted. People feel safe when they know that they can depend upon us to act in a compassionate manner. Peace flows within the dynamics of trustworthiness. Become your greatest expression of loving compassion by maintaining accountability for the energy that you bring into each space.

Life is a joyful experience when we are responsible to ourselves for creating it in a pleasant way. We also are responsible for the co-creation of the life experience for humanity. We either give value to our fellowman through positive living and service to others or we add to the misery of humanity by our negative actions or our lack of care.

Let us, each one, choose for ourselves just how much we want to add to the positive improvement of our living conditions within society. There will be those of us who excel in our contributions and acts of service. It is up to each one of us to do our part in the development of a better world for humanity.

Example

We are all examples to each other by our way of living, our way of being in the world. Our words may be crafted to impress people, but ultimately it is our behavior that makes the greatest impact. A person can fake it only for so long before their actions betray them.

Catch yourself as soon as you fall. Make no excuses for living less than you are capable. Rise to the occasion to provide an example worth emulating. Be the type of person that you wish to be. It is in your hands, literally. You can do it.

Small steps up the mountain will get you there eventually, and as you build upon your strength with each step you will find that it gets easier as you climb, for you are building muscle and stamina. Do not be discouraged if you should falter or scrape your knee. Pull yourself up and continue the journey. Even if you sprain an ankle, resume your climb once you have healed the damage.

Allow your passion and purpose to pull you up the slope. This is easier than having your pain push you all the way to the top. Use ropes to assist your efforts, these can be positive affirmations, a cheerleading section of friends or a helping hand when needed. Rely on your Soul to inspire you with enthusiasm. Your Soul is your greatest asset, it will never fail you. Trust in the innate strength and goodness of your true Self, your Soul Self.

Intention

What is your intention in this life? What purpose do you endeavor to fulfill in your current incarnation? Why have you chosen to come to Earth to live as a human being? Do you know? If so, well done and how are you faring? Are you completing every step necessary to reach your goals? For, one's purpose can be filled with numerous tasks to achieve. How many have you completed so far? Do you need assistance, or maybe someone to hold you accountable? Knowing one's purpose is not the same as fulfilling it.

If you do not yet understand your purpose for this life there are many ways to uncover it from within you. Meditation is our strongest suggestion, for it is held within your Soul's knowing. Develop a rapport with this spiritual aspect that is divine. Allow it to guide you into your life's mission. It is ready and waiting for you to give it the attention needed to communicate with you.

Sometimes it is useful to gain assistance from someone who has been trained by their own Soul to be a guide for the purpose of assisting others into a strong and trusting relationship with their Souls. You will feel when you have found a proper match for yourself. Your Soul will dance with delight when you speak with this helper. Trust yourself to choose wisely based upon how you feel.

Remember though, that your Soul is who you want to develop this relationship of trust with, not the person guiding you to that means. They are only temporary; your relationship with your Soul is permanent. Do not get stuck in dependency upon another human being. Utilize their loving assistance until you can stand strong on your own.

A true coach will release you when the time is right. If they do their job well, you will be empowered to excel beyond their assistance. It is each instructor's desire that his student surpass him. Find a good teacher and endeavor to go beyond their tutoring. Ultimately, your Soul is your master teacher.

Unconditional Love

We are pleased to share with you another gentle reminder of who you really are – LOVE. This means compassion, acceptance and sharing. This is natural to your very BEING. To express less than this is a choice. Are you choosing to express your full divine nature?

It is natural to assist others in need. It is innate within each person to care for another. When one is experiencing joyful passion, all in their presence are positively affected. It is a person's divine nature, their Soul, which shares freely with other Souls.

Where are you holding back your love? What causes you to stop the natural flow of joy? Who prevents you from expressing your passionate nature? Do you permit anything or anyone to interfere with your true loving expression? You are always at choice.

Can you accept your own divine nature? As Spirit, do you realize your worth? Is love your true expression? Does joy permeate your life experience? Is your presence uplifting to others? Do you choose to express your positive feelings freely? Do you wait for someone else to share first? Or, will you share your highest truth, your Self openly? Are you ready to express your true Soul Self?

Have you been able to discern the difference between real, unconditional love and sentimentality? Real love is generated within the heart area (4th chakra). Sentimentality erupts from the belly (3rd chakra). And, lust forms within the sacral area (2nd chakra).

Real Love 4th Chakra	Sentimentality 3rd Chakra	Lust 2nd Chakra
Unconditional	Conditional	Sexual
Current	Past	Chemical/Hormonal
Giving/Sharing	Needy/Taking	Addictive
Highest Good	Selfish Demands	Physical Gratification

Do you desire the highest good for yourself and others? Is sharing with another your ideal? Do you remain current with those you love? Is your love unconditional? So many people fall into the category of sentimentality and use controlling, manipulative ways to guilt or shame others into doing what they want. This false syrupy type of behavior destroys trust and true friendship. Beware of these demeaning tactics.

Cultivate real love in your lives and enjoy the bounty of true camaraderie. We invite you to fearlessly love yourself and others. We encourage you to share with all, authentically, as your true Soul Self.

Your Life's Garden

Have you accepted your divine role in your life? Are you ready to listen within to the guidance of your Soul to create all that you are capable of? Have you begun aligning your ego-mind with your Soul's knowing? Is your relationship with your Self improving?

Life is like a field ready to be planted with your desires. It is up to you to cultivate the ground, your mind, and plant the seeds that will bring you what you most desire to experience. Be sure to weed out what does not belong. Water what you want to grow and nourish each idea you lovingly plant.

If you change your mind and desire something different, then dig up what you no longer want and plant what you do. It is, after all, your garden, your life. What brings you joy? Your life is yours to do with however you choose. And, if you do not make conscious choices, then your life's garden will grow by default. This may include numerous weeds, or even poisonous plants. Your soil may even become barren with only rocks for landscape.

How do you prevent a desolate life? By taking command of your thoughts, feelings and beliefs. By infusing your mind with inspiration from your Soul. By listening within to the nourishing ideas of your own truth, your purpose blueprint. Everyone has been born with a Soul and a blueprint (design) for their current incarnation. This valuable information can be retrieved by communicating with your Soul. Listen deeply to the still small voice within. It is your guiding light.

Cultivate a powerful relationship with your Self – body, ego-mind and Soul. Become your true Self. We call this the Soul Self. As you erase the false programs that interfere with your creativity, you will unleash the power of Spirit within to your awakened divinity.

What goals are you cultivating in your life's garden? Have you planned out the entire season or maybe even the next 10 years? Remember, you will only harvest that which you plant and cultivate. (Default is less than desirable.)

Are you utilizing everything in Nature to bring forth a prosperous harvest? Is your soil fertile? Does your garden receive enough water? Is the irrigation system working well? Do you have a back-up water supply? Do you use high quality natural fertilizer? Is there enough sunshine to accelerate growth? Are you removing the weeds that suck the life away from your vegetation?

Seeds – Thoughts, ideas, beliefs
Soil – Mind
Water – Positive emotion, feeling, desire
Irrigation – Discipline, patience and certainty
Back-up Water Supply – Key desires that are backed with passion
Fertilizer – Inspiration, positive information
Sunshine – Passion, enthusiasm, dedication, diligence, conviction
Weeds – That which chokes, covers over or interferes with positive growth and expression (false beliefs, negative thoughts, manipulative people, etc.)

Now that you have become a gardener of your life, will you diligently take care of your field? Will you plant high quality seeds? Will you weed regularly? Will you grow organic, wholesome vegetation? Are you prepared to complete the harvest once your ideas have come to fruition? Do you have enough people and resources to fully reap the bounty of your flourishing harvest? Be prepared. "You reap what you sow."

Empathy

What does it mean to be fully human? Ponder this for a while.

NOW is a good time to change your idea of yourself as a separate individual into a higher view as an interconnected Being. Humans have within their make-up four major aspects – animal instinct, logical mind, empathic emotions, and spiritual intuition. Combined and working in unison, these aspects create a well-rounded view of life. Utilize all of your abilities to decipher for yourself the best action to take in any given circumstance.

Do you feel compassion for all life? Fellow feeling is an empathic connection to the happenings of another. Understanding comes easily when one can feel what another is experiencing (Though caution must be used in order not to get caught up in the drama of the other). To understand another assists a person to have compassion. Yet, compassion does not see the other as a victim, but rather, as a person of ignorance.

Wisdom is available to all. Each Soul is endowed with the ability to access their inner truth which will dissolve the discord within the ego-mind, thereby erasing inner and outer conflict. Peace comes from compassionate understanding. Have you become aware of the interconnected world of God where everything affects everything? Does your empathic nature assist you in understanding other people? Does this compassion bring you closer to your brothers and sisters?

Are you ready to live your life as a fully interconnected Being, as within, so without, with all of humanity?

Discernment

What is your favorite color? Is it the best of all that is available? Does someone else's choice differ from yours? How do you prove which is better? Can you?

We hope this very simple test has shown you that opinion is relative. There is no law that states that one color is greater or better than another. Now apply this to EVERYTHING.

How many years of age must one be to know oneself? Is 50 a safe guess? How about 75? Or would you be closer to being accurate if you said 2? When did you forget? Or stop allowing yourself to fully express? And, why? Did society's programming overtake your natural expression and make you think, act and believe like everyone else?

It is time to take back your Soul authority which is your birthright. Listen to your own inner voice that wants to free itself from the dungeons of mediocrity. Express your own inner truth without fear of condemnation from false authority figures outside of yourself. Awaken to your own divinity.

What does spirituality mean? Is it following daily, weekly, monthly, or yearly rituals? Who proclaimed these ritualistic acts as spiritual? If one does not follow these specific rites are they less spiritual than one who does? How do you base your opinion? God is ALL THAT IS, meaning that everything is spiritual, even inanimate objects. For, to say that something is not of God is in opposition to God being ALL. How then can you judge?

How many times must one fail before they change their minds? Are you a quick learner? Or, do you need to beat your head against a wall until you are bloodied before looking within for a better way? Society has continued down a road that leads to failure, unrest, injustice, aggravation and dismay. Why do people continue doing that which obviously does not work? Why aren't people thinking of ways to improve their lives, and then implementing them? What great FEAR holds back the majority of the population from attaining greatness, happiness and fulfillment?

FEAR OF CONDEMNATION

Who is courageous enough to break free of this false ego-mindset? Are you? We will help you. There is no judge appointed by THE ALL. People make judgments, not THE ALL. How can ALL THAT IS make a judgment that is not against itself? Are you judging yourself or anyone else?

Solution: Choose to replace **judgment** against another with **discernment** for oneself. This will eliminate every issue, guaranteed! What is the difference between discernment and judgment?

Discernment	Judgment
Is this something for my good?	This is 'bad' for everyone and must be banned.
Will acting on this bring about highest good for all?	This action is EVIL and must be punished.
I choose to express love and harmony.	They are wicked and in need of chastisement.
I can allow others to choose for themselves.	I must dictate what is right for all.
I will invite another to consider a different choice.	I will condemn another for poor choices.
Self-Responsibility	Meddling in another's affairs.

Which do you choose?

Diversity will look evermore wondrous as you release your programmed judgments and repressions. Look at each person you meet as your sister or brother, and begin living in community consciousness. Become aware of your connection with everything and everyone. Invite your heart to share in the feeling of connection. We hope that you will allow yourself to change your perceptions as you experience greater evidence of life being DIVINE.

Equivalence

Do you believe in the equivalence of ALL life? WE do. WE are no more important than you are. WE only vibrate at a higher level because of our understanding. WE would be honored for you to join our level of frequency. Because, where two or more are gathered (in consciousness) there you will find connection, belonging, understanding, fellow camaraderie.

Please join us in our endeavor to assist humanity to raise their consciousness high enough to live in love, harmony and good feeling. Everything is GOD, yet there are certain lower vibrations that create an uncomfortable feeling within the human psyche. We prefer to allow these vibrations to inhabit other worlds that are still learning about choice.

Earth and humanity are now ready to elevate their consciousness to bring forth abundance and joy for everyone. Please join forces with those who speak out to conquer the illusions of FEAR, created by false beliefs involving judgment and condemnation.

Know this: GOD CONDEMNS NOTHING, for that would mean condemning itself – ALL THAT IS.

As you progress in your uncovering of yourself, you will come to see just how influenced you have been throughout your life. You will catch the false ideas that make no real sense to divine beings. How can you inhibit the flow of life-force energy and still remain whole?

Where have these ideas of restriction come from? Would an all-powerful Being, God, create magnificence and then condemn their creation for expressing itself completely? Would you give your child a painting kit filled with 50 colors, and yet demand that they only use 3, with a threat of punishment for disobedience? Would that make sense to you?

Common sense tells you that everything is of God, ALL THAT IS. You must discern for yourself what is in your own best interest, and for all of creation. If you desire to make a product that would eliminate stains from fabric make sure that it does not bring harm to the environment. If you desire to create a sugar substitute, make sure it is not harmful to the body. Do you understand the principle? Have fun creating everything for your pleasure, for the benefit of every living entity, and for the well-being of the Earth.

Now that you have been introduced to your true identity as divine beings, we would like to have you adjust your thinking to include everything as a reflection of consciousness, or belief. What does your experience of life on Earth reveal to you about your current state of consciousness?

We would like to bring you into the confident knowing of your own authority as a co-creator of your individual life experience, as well as your role in the collective consciousness of humanity during this time on Earth. Be still and know that YOU are God, along with everyone else. What type of creator will you be? Will you raise your awareness to perceive all of life, beyond what your physical senses can see? Are you ready to be completely responsible for your thought creations?

Choose now to be accountable for every thought, feeling and belief that registers within your mind. Dismiss nothing that stirs a reaction within you. Learn to 'see' the origin of every experience in your life. This is how you will become the MASTER of your life experience.

Mystical Mind

There is a fascination with mysticism that people tend to lean towards. It makes sense when you realize that EVERYTHING is mystical. We mean that everything begins within the mind as thought before it becomes material. The mystical world is the arena where things are made in MIND prior to becoming an object that can be touched or a concept that can be conceived and put into practice. It all begins within the mind.

What are you formulating within your mind right now? Is it a new thought or one that has been thought before? Very few people think new thoughts. This is a shame, because there are so many wonderful thoughts that haven't been thought yet. We have assisted mankind for many centuries to come up with better ways of living. It has been a challenge to keep people on track with Nature, because of greed. Greed causes people to think selfish thoughts that eventually bring destruction to their environment. We hope humanity will wake up soon to the fact that they are responsible for their own demise. But, it is not too late to turn things around, to work in cooperation with the natural flow of the Universe and all living Beings.

We suggest that you spend time alone with your Soul, your spiritual inner voice, inner sight and inner knowing. It is this spiritual aspect of yourself that will pull you out of the danger zone that your ego-mind has allowed you to fall into. Realize that your Soul has all of the answers that you seek. It will open the doors to your good. Ask and it will guide you back to your knowing.

We offer our assistance to you, and this assistance is encouraging you to wake up to YOURSELF. Become your Soul Self, which is your true identity as a human being. Seek out your Soul's guidance. It will show you the way. Awaken your fascination with your Mystical Mind.

Signs of Nature

There are so many ways to interpret your world. Clues can be found within every word used by your mind. Numbers have codes within them that when interpreted correctly can assist you to make wise decisions. The planets hold their form by utilizing the forces of Nature and many people have delved into the interpretation using Astrology to uncover bits of information that is available for everyone.

Because everything is energy, everything vibrates with particular frequency codes or information. Science likes to break it down, but we suggest that you keep your focus on the WHOLE of life, for everything communicates in your world, EVERYTHING.

Would you not like to be informed by your consciousness of everything that would aid you in co-creating what you desire? Why would you want to limit your knowledge? Who has decreed that understanding the world of consciousness is 'bad'? "Seek and you shall find" is a scripture encouraging you to do just that – to seek out what you need in order to fulfill your desire.

We would like to also encourage you to overcome your false beliefs of fear, because fear will only keep you in the darkness. Come into the LIGHT of knowledge and wisdom. Your Soul knows all things. This spiritual aspect of yourself is connected to Source energy, ALL THAT IS. Within your Soul's blueprint is the reason why you have chosen to incarnate here on Earth at this time. 99% of your role will have something to do with bringing Earth and its inhabitants back into balance. We know this because this is the aim of nearly every living Being at this time. We all desire to save planet Earth from the destruction created by man's ego-mind foolhardy ideas that cause separation from the unity of The ALL.

Come back into ONENESS now. Utilize all of the information available to you by learning how to interpret the signs of Nature. Open your hearts to feel what is best for bringing balance and unity back to planet Earth. It is in your hands to clean up your mess.

Help or Harm?

How do you know what is for your good? Can you rely upon the opinions of others? Is there a sure fire way of knowing for yourself? We say, "Yes, there is!" Your Soul has access to everything that you will need in this lifetime to fulfill your purpose. Rely upon your Soul's understanding, for it will guide you correctly.

Some people call this the conscience, but we know that the conscience is just a mechanism of the mind that can be tricked by the ego world into believing that even things that are good for you are somehow 'bad.' We do not use the word, 'bad' for several reasons. One is that there is no such thing, because it is ALL GOD, therefore, ALL GOOD. Two, it is all relative. For instance, a knife can be used for cutting rope or bringing harm to another. The knife is not good or bad, it just is. How a person uses that knife is either to help or to harm. Third, sometimes it is necessary to do something that seems bad in order to bring about highest good. Take the birth of a child, it may seem terrible during the painful childbirth process, but the end result is positively glorious.

You have developed many technologies that seem to help people to live an easier life, yet many of your inventions have caused great harm and upheaval to the balance of life. Many of your creations have caused illness and even extinction to certain species. Yet, you name them 'good.' We would call them 'ignorant devices of harm.' Nature has within it all that one needs to know to keep the balance of life. Greed for money, lust for power and laziness have created numerous tools of destruction. We hope that you will go back to the basics of true living, with Nature as your instructor and your Soul as your guide.

Back to Nature

Nature runs on automatic. Our bodies also operate automatically, as long as we do our part to nourish and cleanse ourselves. Every part of life is a hologram. We are as infinite and as finite as anything in the Universe. Everything is interconnected to the minutest detail. Just because we cannot see it with our physical eyes does not mean that it is not true. It just means that we have forgotten how to 'see'.

Intuition is our tool for understanding the complexities of life that are actually really simple. There is a flow to the Universe and we are either IN the flow or not. Life flows forward. Death does not flow. You can choose to enter into the flow of life or you can choose to stop yourself from flowing, and eventually your body would expire. Life-force energy is found in organic soil, organic food, living water and clean air. Pollution stops the flow of life and stifles the flow of Nature. When you breathe in these toxins, your body begins to die. When you drink polluted water, your body begins to die. When you eat poisoned food, your body begins to die. Why would you choose to do this?

We recommend that you get back to Nature as quickly as you can. Your survival depends upon it. Actually, the survival of all living Beings made of Earth depends upon it. The Earth itself will swing back to balance when either YOU (humanity) make course corrections or after your extinction. The choice is yours.

Abundance

How does the Earth multiply its living resources? It does so abundantly, persistently, and without fail. Nature is our model for sustainability. When we rely on Nature's way, we are assured ABUNDANCE! Nature uses life-force energy to create from itself, multiplied. One seed can create thousands. One male joined with one female of most species can multiply themselves. Life is abundant.

Why has man endeavored to dominate over others by creating scarcity? Genetically modified organisms do not create more viable seeds. These plants must be engineered by man and sold for profit. They are not grown naturally by God. This creates a scarcity consciousness whereby man is dependent upon commercial industries to supply their food. God created food that can be shared with all without cost. One apple can grow many trees. Seeds can be saved from each crop to proliferate into more.

When will mankind say, "Enough!"? When will people rise up to save themselves from big business? When will the Earth be revered for her bounty? When will YOU take back your authority and come into balance with Nature?

The sustainability movement is humanity's way back into alignment with Nature, God and our dear home, the Earth. What role are you playing in bringing back Nature's way?

Ideas

There are many ideas out in the ethers. How many will come to completion? Maybe 10%? That would be a monumental accomplishment. If you brought to fruition every idea you ever contemplated, would you have time to sleep? Probably not. We would like you to know that even if you accomplished 1% of your thoughts you would be considered a superstar.

So, of the 99.5% that you do not complete, which ones would you prefer to put your attention on in order to materialize? We suggest that you think on this for a while because every idea takes action, and every action takes time, and there is only so much time in your life-span. Consider wisely.

Of the ideas you choose to put into action, which ones benefit the whole of creation? Will they bring prosperity to others? Will your ideas maintain balance within the eco-system? Will they enhance the joy of humanity? Will they bring forth more love and fulfillment in your life, and in the lives of those around you? These are the things that are most beneficial to put your time into. Think on these things, and build up yourself and others with constructive ideas brought to fruition.

Reincarnation

How many thoughts can a person entertain within one lifetime? Is it fathomable to think that a human being can fulfill every wish within the 70 or 80 years of their life? Would it not make more sense to have numerous lifetimes by which to carry out every desire? This is what many traditions call reincarnation.

There are people who remember their lives from their past. There have been studies and research into phenomena that seem to prove the validity of reincarnation. What is your take on it? Do you find it odd to live only three quarters of a century with all that life has to offer? Or do you sense that there is more than this single incarnation?

We would offer to you a simple process: Take a few minutes to become still within yourself. Center your awareness within your heart area. Breathe deeply and slowly. Relax. Can you feel the core of your Self? We call this your Soul. It is your spiritual essence. It communicates with you through intuition, feeling, instinct, visions, dreams, that still small voice within, and through your nervous system. Allow enough time to commune with your Soul until you develop a knowing of its presence.

Now, ask it to bring forth answers to your life's questions. Be prepared to understand intuitively what it is sharing with you. As you develop this relationship with your essence, your Soul, you will most likely become the best of friends. This is good because, in reality, this aspect of you is your truest friend. It has been with you for eons of time. It knows you better than anyone could. All of your answers are within you, held within your Soul's knowing. Become acquainted with your true Self, and endeavor to work with your Soul to accomplish all of your true desires.

Activation of Blueprint

The activation of one's blueprint is what occurs when we find our true purpose for this incarnation. It is simple, really. How can we deny ourselves of the reason we were born? This would only lead to disappointment, disillusionment and depression. Are you feeling any of these feelings now? Are you unsure of your proper role as a human being? We would like to offer assistance.

Ask deep within yourself what feels right to you. What would create a sense of fulfillment and joy in your life? Are you living your life on purpose? Do you have a plan? Does it cover all of your needs and desires? Are you willing to do the work necessary to accomplish it? Do you get up each morning with enthusiasm to get started? Does it have enough pizzazz to keep your focus? Do you feel it is attainable?

If you are having doubts, spend more time alone. Develop a dialog with your Soul and ask for more guidance. Ask for ways to strengthen your faith in the goodness of life. Ask your Soul to reveal to you how you can improve your attitude. Become a master asker. Your Soul has all of the answers to your questions, and will gladly share them with you. All you need is to have a listening ear.

How can you serve your Soul? How can you promote better living for humanity? What can you do to bring balance back to planet Earth? How can you make a difference in this world? Service is the key. Whenever we serve the highest good of another, we serve the highest good of all. Your blueprint will be 50% the same as all human beings. That is; we are all here to co-create joy, well-being, abundance and camaraderie.

The other 50% is unique to you. This is where you will find your passion. This is what excites your Soul. Search within your memory banks to uncover the times when you felt completely alive. What brought you a feeling of true and lasting satisfaction? When did you ignite your enthusiasm so greatly that you lost track of time? These are clues to where your attention should go for these are the things that wake you from your slumber. Wake yourself up with the fire within your Soul. Your blueprint will burn bright when it is activated.

Create A Better Life

What are you willing to do to make your life better? Do you need to wake up earlier in the morning to have more time? Do you need to get to bed at a decent hour? Would eating healthier, whole foods improve how you feel? Would you improve your attitude if you watched more positive television shows? Could you cut down on the amount of TV you watch each week?

Would spending more time with people you care about increase your joy? How about going for a walk alone, with a friend, or with your dog? What do you think you need to improve your life? What do you feel would bring forth more happiness? Get clear on what it is you can do to create a better life for yourself, and then do it. Your Soul awaits your conviction.

Once you make a decision, the Universe begins to bring to you all that you need to accomplish your task. Your Soul will open the doors that will manifest your desires. Your part is to COMMIT. Make a decision, and use your will power to accomplish your goal. Work with your Soul's aspirations for a joyful life. Decide now.

Make Your Voice Heard

We are fully capable as human beings to create the world that we desire. Everyone has the same basic needs: sunshine, clean air, pure water, nutrient rich soil, nutritious food, proper shelter and true companionship. These must become first priority within society for there to be contentment among the masses. Then, there will be time for individuals to co-create their secondary needs, which are joy, fulfillment, purpose, passion and creativity. After these have been obtained, one will feel at peace with the world that they have assisted in co-creating.

How many of these needs have you fulfilled? How is the governing system in your country providing for your well-being? If you are less than satisfied, then become active in changing the current situation. It is your country wherever you are a citizen; therefore, it is your right to demand changes for the better. How active a role do you play within the system? Make your voice heard. Inform people of the necessary changes for their well-being. Take charge of your life.

Love or Fear?

Everything in your life is a by-product of your current consciousness. YOU are in charge of your circumstances. Yes, YOU are co-creating every moment of every day. Change where you are creating from and you will change your life. Are you creating from love or fear?

Creating from fear resembles a sick dog giving birth to a litter of weak pups. People who create from a place of lack only create more scarcity. A person who acts out of fear of punishment is not acting from integrity. People who cheat, lie and deceive are coming from a negative place within their consciousness. Dishonor comes from a lack of honor. Weakness begets weakness. Examine where you are weak, and make the necessary changes to strengthen your integrity.

When you come from a place of strength you create positive outcomes. Strength begets strength. Utilize your conviction to remain pure of heart, and create from this foundation. This is where true purpose can be accomplished for the betterment of yourself and all of humanity. Create from LOVE, compassion, and desire for the well-being of everyone. Love is active. It takes courage to live in integrity. Strengthen your courage to live FOR the betterment of your world. Take positive action to create the changes needed to improve life for all!

Change

Life is change in all of its stages. There is a natural order to the Universe, and change is its constant. When we see the beauty in change, rather than fearing it, we come to understand how simple life truly is. Examine the cycle of a plant. It begins as a seed, grows into its destiny, creates more seeds of its kind, and eventually decays, becoming soil for its offspring. This cycle keeps plant life in circulation.

Humans have a cycle of life that begins with conception and birth. Children grow into adulthood when they become fertile to procreate their species. With maturity comes the final stage of imparting wisdom to their future generations before expiring. Everything follows a natural cycle in life.

Do not fear what is meant to be beautiful. Each stage has its own beauty. Seek to understand. Endeavor to experience all that life has to offer within each phase. Celebrate wherever you find yourself within this Universal cycle of life.

Everything is Good

Why do you think that there is such a thing as bad? What can be said to be separate from God? What kind of thing can be separated from ALL THAT IS? Logically, you will understand that NOTHING can be separate from THE ALL. Therefore, nothing can be considered as bad.

This concept of good and bad has caused many hardships among people. It causes separation among brothers and sisters. It creates wars among nations. It prevents life-force energy from naturally flowing through our bodies, creating illness and disease. It is time to wake up from this slumbering thought system that denies reality.

Reality is; everything is consciousness. Everything is interconnected. Everything is a part of the WHOLE of existence. EVERYTHING IS GOD. Therefore, everything is good. Find the good in everything you would name as bad. If you open your heart to see through the eyes of LOVE, you will be able to find the cause behind the thing in question, and you will come to understand that whatever formulated this thing was created with the energy of life, which is good.

Bad is just a concept used to create a sense of separation from the whole, in order to weaken a person to surrender their authority to someone else. WAKE UP! There is no authority outside of you. You are just as much God material as anything else. It is up to you how much you choose to behave like God, for in God's image you were made. BE GOD NOW.

What Are You Afraid Of?

When you wake up in the morning, do you decide to make the best of your day? Do you set out to accomplish tasks that would bring you closer to your ideal? Are you productive with your time? Have you written out a plan that you follow in order to reach your goals? And, do your goals include improving life for yourself and all of Earth's inhabitants?

If your answer is yes, that is very good. You will enjoy your life, and you will find purpose in everything that you do. Your days will be filled with action, accomplishment and celebration. You will make a difference in this world.

If your answer was no, why is that? What prevents you from designing a plan to bring to yourself all that you desire in life? Where is your motivation to get up in the morning? What is blocking your natural creativity? What has caused you to shut down the flow of life-force energy within your body? What keeps your mind in this state of slumber? Why do you not take action to better your life, or that of others?

The answer is FEAR. Fear blocks the natural flow of LOVE, interfering with our natural state of well-being. When love is lacking, life is lacking. What are you afraid of? IT IS ALL GOD. Why are you afraid of God? Could it be that you have been taught to fear God by the religion you were raised in? Does this make any sense to you? Remember that everything taught to us comes through the minds and mouths of human beings. People teach us from their perspectives and personal views. They relate through the filters of their perception. And, man is fallible.

It is time to stop believing the stories of others, and the falsehoods that have been perpetuated for centuries by tradition. Our thoughts should not be regulated by man. We are free moral agents. We each have a mind of our own. Nature is our greatest teacher, for from Nature we are made. And, Nature is God's way. Wake up, and listen within to your Soul. It will teach you truth. Trust your Soul.

Mature Wisdom

Have you seen the beneficial results of living a mature life? Have you brought into manifestation all that you have conceptualized from the inspiration of your Soul? Have you put into practice the art of completing what you have committed yourself to? Do your values show themselves in your work ethic? Have you matured yourself to the point of taking appropriate actions to accomplish your goals? Have you reaped a good harvest from your dedicated mental thought process and the required physical action that is necessary in order to bring your cultivated spiritual seedlings into full bloom to fulfill your purpose?

If so, are you teaching others by your example? Have you decided to assist people further through workshops, personal coaching or by writing a how-to book?

If not, what are you lacking? What keeps your energy blocked from manifesting your ideals? Who are you waiting for to do it for you, and why? Where is the maturity to take full responsibility to co-create the life you came here to live? Have you figured out what your Soul's purpose is for this incarnation? And, why are you behind in fulfilling your purpose?

Seek within for your answers. Learn from those who have mastered their goals. Take the appropriate action to complete what you have decided upon. Spend time creating your desired outcome within the miraculous tool of your imagination. See it within your mind's eye. Feel it in the cells of your body. Experience it as already done. And, know for certain that it must now complete. This is the wisdom of Nature. Decide what seed to plant, take the action, cultivate it to maturity, and reap the harvest.

It is that simple.

Harvesting

What have you been harvesting in your life so far? Are you pleased with your results? Do you feel fulfilled in your life thus far? How many goals have you achieved? Has your purpose for this incarnation become clearer? Are you ready to bring everything into fruition?

Let's get started. First, what have you uncovered from your Soul's knowing? How many facets are involved within your purpose? What is the designated time frame that you endeavor to achieve these goals? Have you procured for yourself the tools necessary to accomplish them, such as, acquiring knowledge and experience, proper funding, adequate time, fellow co-creators, etc.?

Second, now that you are clear, are you congruent? Does your ego-mind support your Soul's aspirations? Is your body ready to take the necessary action? Are you in agreement with your purpose – mentally, emotionally, physically and spiritually? Or, does your subconscious sabotage your results? This needs to be dealt with before you can proceed with any type of success. Find the incongruence's within you and master them. Then, move on to phase three.

Third, as a congruent whole, write out your plan. Place benchmarks, time frames, tools needed, people required, and your total commitment. Map out your crop, your mission. Begin with the basic foundation and then fill in the details. Be sure to commit to each step that you put into writing.

Fourth, take the appropriate actions to fulfill your purpose. Follow your plan, while remaining flexible. Adapt to changing circumstances, and never quit.

Finally, experience the fulfilling results of reaping the benefits of your well-designed and completed harvest. Enjoy your life to the fullest. Congratulations! You have succeeded in fulfilling your Soul's purpose. Well done.

Where Are You Creating From?

How is your soil? Is it nutrient rich? How deep is it? How large is your field? Check within to decipher how well you are receiving and giving unconditional love, wisdom, joy and compassion. Examine your life to see how you are experiencing and expressing these qualities. Improve your soil and you will improve the harvest.

Are you receptive to spiritual wealth? Have you developed a strong line of communication with your Soul? Do you radiate a positive attitude and share it with others? "By their fruits you will recognize them" is a saying that shows just how well our lives can be compared to growing a garden. How spiritually rich is the soil of your consciousness?

Spirituality is not the same as religious. It matters not whether you belong to a form of religion. Everyone is spiritual according to the degree of their developed consciousness. Some have developed a stronger degree than others. Yet, all are spiritual because we all originate from Spirit. How strong have you developed yourself up to now? Are you pleased? Or, do you desire to grow more?

Your life is created by your level of consciousness. Where are you creating from? Do you endeavor to force what you want through control over others? Realize that this is a lower frequency that eventually will back-fire because the ego-mind is too limited to bring forth any real fulfillment in life. Do you use tactics of manipulation to coerce others into giving to you out of pity? This ego-mind drama is short-lived, as people will tire of your victim consciousness.

Or, have you matured yourself to the point of realization that you are here to fulfill the purpose of your Soul's incarnation? This is where true success lies. Your Soul is the spiritual aspect of your being. It is already of high vibration because it is solely connected to Source. As you become more of your true essence, you grow into living your Soul Self life. Creating from here is what the masters have been teaching for years.

Check your soil to see how fertile your consciousness is for cultivating a life that ripens into fulfillment. Always be aware of where you are creating from. Deepen your understanding, widen your expanse and increase your spiritual loving nature. Become a nutrient rich soil capable of growing a spiritually abundant life.

Manifestation

It is becoming clear to many that this world is fluid. Thoughts turn into things. Ideas convert into reality. Change occurs when one's perception shifts, causing doors to open where there were once walls.

Have you had the experience of seemingly miraculous coincidences showing up in a most timely manner? When you thought there was no way through, a miracle occurred? Have you experienced some of your childhood daydreams coming into fruition, fulfilling former desires that you had forgotten about?

These are 'seeds' that have finally germinated and come to fruition. Every heartfelt desire is a seed that has been planted, and eventually will take root. You may speed up the growth by coming into alignment with your desire. This is best accomplished within your feeling nature. Really FEEL your desire as already happening. And then, it must occur.

Practice this technique regularly and you will be amazed at just how speedy your desires come into manifestation.

Creatorship

God is a word we use to define the position of Creator. As those who are made in the 'image of God,' we humans also carry within us the ability to create our experience in life. And, together, humans co-create their world. What are people co-creating that brings goodwill to all? How often do our creations serve all of humanity & all of life on Earth? What improvements can we make to bring back the full, natural rhythm of life?

The destiny of humanity is in our own hands. Will we learn from Nature soon enough to avoid foolishly co-creating our own demise? Will we prevent the extinction of our kind before it is too late? How serious are we about turning ourselves around from the seemingly inevitable doom created by our greed?

Life is teeming with possibility. Abundance exists within the natural flow of the Universe. Earth exists within certain Universal laws that can be utilized for greater living. Are you ready to uncover your own natural rhythm to help support the re-establishment of balance within Nature? What are you personally doing now to assist life on Earth to flourish again? Is it enough? Or, can you do better?

Be Fertile Soil

Your level of consciousness will determine the fertility of your creations. Make sure that you are cultivating the proper drainage for your 'soil', so that you do not become a swamp-filled land that only fosters crocodiles, snakes and hippos. These types of 'creatures' represent destruction to your fields of fruitage.

Bring your excess 'water' (emotions) into the creek that leads to the ocean. Cry your tears, and then dry your eyes. Do not stay stuck in the pain, drowning yourself into a swamp. Allow yourself the necessary time to grieve, a week, or a month should suffice for anything that troubles you. Be sure to move forward with life when the grieving period is over.

Also, be sure to irrigate your land with good feeling emotion. Get into the best feeling you can when you contemplate your future. Create with as much positive feeling as you can sustain, always endeavoring to expand your positive attitude. This alone will increase your yield more than many hours of hard labor. FEEL GOOD = successful harvest.

Positive Emotion

Positive emotion is valuable beyond measure. It is worth more than silver or gold. For, with positive emotion you can create whatever your Soul delights in. When you come to understand truly that all things material begin first in the spiritual realm of thought and feeling, you will know just how valuable positive emotion is for creating a positive life.

A sculptor can create from marble or clay. If he desires to have a lasting creation he will most likely choose the marble as his material. This may take him longer to develop his masterpiece, but it will not crumble to pieces when bumped by the hard knocks of life.

Choose wisely the proper materials for the job. Take the time needed to develop your sculpture properly, so you will be able to enjoy it for the rest of your incarnation.

Life Sustains Life

Do you have a strong, positive character? Are you courageous in protecting your Soul's purpose for this incarnation? Is honesty your highest value? Does your passion include compassion for others? Do you feel connected to all of life, thereby treating every living being with reverence?

How strong are you adhering to the principles of virtue? Is your integrity to that of the highest good of all? Do you take into consideration the divinity and sacredness of all life? Without exception, every living being is divine, and of God. This does not necessarily mean that life should not be given for that of another. All creatures must eat to sustain themselves, whether herbivore, carnivore, or omnivore. Life exists to sustain life.

Living plants feed the majority of creatures. Each species has their place within the 'circle of life.' Humans seem to be at the top of this chain, but they are not exempt from becoming food for certain wild creatures. This is all part of the cycle. Do not judge LIFE. It is all sacred.

Divine Expression

Have you been able to accept your connection to ALL THAT IS? Is your awareness opening to the divinity of life? Can you allow yourself to BE divine?

The world co-created here on Earth is a mixture of Nature, divinity and the ego-mind belief system. When you can focus your attention on Nature, God's way, you come to recognize everything as divine. When you can overcome the limitations you have unwittingly accepted from the false perceptions of the ego-mind, you will inevitably express divinity.

All restrictions are from this ego world for the purpose of limiting your God expression, or divinity. Separation from the Oneness of ALL THAT IS, or God, is what the ego-mind belief systems are all about. Choose to break free from these false teachings of limitation, and express your divinity, your natural God-expression of Life.

Agreement

You will eventually come to realize that everything in your experience has come forth due to a frequency match within your energy field. Somewhere in your experience you have had a thought, or idea that formulated this event. It could have been created from a movie that you watched as a child, a story that was read to you or a belief that was shared with you from your parents or other people that you held in esteem. However it entered your consciousness, you have recreated it for your own experience.

You can change any idea that you no longer wish to experience. A powerful formula is this: create a new belief to replace this old one. A belief is made from the combination of a mental thought, emotional reaction and an agreement. Here is an example of changing a belief. Let's say you were taught that dancing was bad. The people who helped you to 'program' this belief within you shared with strong emotion that to dance was acting in a way that was harmful to you and others. They felt so strongly about this idea that it frightened you, so you accepted this to be true. Now, you see differently. You want to change this belief to that of the teaching that to move one's body to music is a sign of reverence and appreciation for the gift of life and well-being. Muster as much feeling and emotion as possible, because it is the 'energy in motion' that will cancel out the old formula, and replace it with this new idea that you are in agreement.

To change a belief, you must overcome the old fearful emotion with a greater positive one. Thought + feeling = belief. If you were scared into a belief, you must muster the courage to decide differently. Logic alone cannot change a die-hard belief. Emotion is what locks it into place. Overcome your fear with faith in LOVE. IT IS ALL GOD, therefore, it is all LOVE in differing degrees. Choose to interpret your life experience from the higher knowing that everything comes from the energy of GOD, created by your agreement, or belief.

Sociality

How social are you? Do you register others as your brothers and sisters? Or, do you think of people as strangers to be leery of or avoided? Where does your way of believing come from; your parents, your religion, your educational system, or the society that you were raised in?

Will you seek true camaraderie with honest folks? Will you develop your integrity to the point necessary to gain the respect and trust of others? Do you take into account all of the diverse ways that God chooses to express, and allow yourself to join with those of like-mind?

There is more 'good' in the world, than what may be considered 'bad.' Can you reach deep enough within yourself to experience it? Endeavor to see past the initial angst of this world system, to experience the beauty of LIFE. Nature remains our greatest teacher of all things God. Learn from this great example. The ego-world is small in comparison to the reality of God, of Nature. Open your heart to see.

God-Given Power

Do you consider yourself to be an honest person? It certainly takes courage to stand firm in your knowing when it seems to clash with the belief system of those who hold an opposing view. Enlightenment comes when the light of truth shines brightly, without dimming its conviction.

How much conviction do you carry for your beliefs? Have you tested them out to the fullest extent available? Or, do you still have some doubt due to inconclusive evidence? Why hold on to beliefs that clearly are not based upon the reality of truth and divinity? When a belief tells you that you are less than divine, what keeps you hanging on to such a lie?

You are made "in the image of God." If you believe this statement, then how can you play small? Make God proud. Show just how much you are willing to be and express this image of greatness. Claim your power now. You carry within you the God-given power of divinity.

Time

We live in a world that uses the concept of time as a reference point from which to base our beliefs. This time factor is actually an illusion that seems very real to us. It keeps us 'on track' in this ego-mind world. When we enter the place within us where time does not exist, we call it Soul. Our Soul space is interconnected with ALL THAT IS in all time, or no time. From here we can 'foresee' multiple possibilities to choose from.

Once we make a decision, time collapses into that expression, and the game begins. That is, the game of creation. It all hinges on decision. When we do not make our own decision, then it falls to default, or the strongest belief within us.

When our underlying belief is 'for us,' we will fare well. When that belief is 'against us,' we will fare poorly. Many beliefs in this ego-mind world have turned us against ourselves, and each other, such as the belief in judgment, condemnation and punishment for actions that are contrary to what we believe at the time are correct. When we learn of the accuracy of a new belief (like the world is round) then we change our minds and no longer judge, condemn or punish people for their belief.

If we all were to remove judgment from our belief system, our world would progress extremely fast. We would no longer act against ourselves or anyone else for trying new things. This is where we are heading; charting new territory for our creations.

Endeavor to go deep within yourself to the place where your Soul resides, outside of the concept of time, and allow yourself to enter non-judgment. From here, you will experience greater truth.

True Power

Joy, the elixir of life, carries within it one of the most well kept secrets to living well. It is true power. Throughout the ages, those who have sought to gain power over another have done so by robbing them of their natural expression of joy. When a person is restricted in their freedom of expression their joy wanes. Guilt, shame and judgment have been tools used to control the masses.

Saints and Gurus have long known that to live in bliss, joy, is the way to total freedom. A person who has found their divinity cannot be controlled by another. Therefore, their joy cannot be restricted because it is founded on the truth of their very Being. And, no one, and nothing can remove this from them.

Fear is the greatest controller known to man. And yet, fear is only an illusion of the ego-mind world. It does not exist within the reality of divinity. Find your joy, your true power within your Soul, and use it to create a better life for yourself, and a better world with others.

Activism

Are you a full participant in life? Do you take action, or do you sit on the sidelines as a spectator? Co-creation is an active process. The current world has been co-created by those who have chosen to act upon their desires. Some of these have brought good to their fellow man. Other ideas have created harm for all living creatures. When the latter occurs, it is important to bring back Nature's balance so that life may continue for all. We have named this role – Activism.

Life is meant to thrive, and it is up to each one of us to maintain the proper balance of Nature for the continuation of our species, as well as for all of creation. How active are you in keeping Nature's balance flowing in your life? Do you grow and eat organic food? Do you use natural ingredients to clean items? Do you use preventative measures to avoid polluting this beautiful planet? Can you improve upon your 'footprint?'

There comes a time when we must take drastic measures to ensure the well-being of all. Find within your heart the courage to stand up for the good of Earth and all of her inhabitants.

Peace

Peace has been sought by many throughout the ages. It is quite simple really. Divinity is peace. Divinity is the understanding that one is God, all is God, and therefore, there is no authority over another. Consciousness naturally plays out as each one believes.

One who has found the depth within their Soul has no need to power over another. They simply allow their consciousness to organize according to their true desire, and all falls into place. The game of the ego-mind world is a childish power play displayed by those who are ignorant of their divinity. It is time for people to awaken their Soul's true authority, their divinity.

Peace will reign on Earth when divinity is achieved within each person. Raise your consciousness to the level of your Soul, your divinity, and live your Soul Self life.

Play

We are designed to play. Life is designed to be joyful. When we enter into the natural flow of life everything is pleasing to our senses. Nature hikes have been known by many to recover our innate knowing of bliss. We tend to relax and revel in Nature's wonderful embrace.

As Nature is encroached upon by man-made systems; illness, dis-ease and stress creep further into our lives. The ego-mind world has developed harmful practices that rob us from our natural state of well-being. We can counter these ill-producing results by remaining in our connection to Nature.

When we play within Nature with living, breathing organisms, we share life-force energy that is a natural healer. Technology alone, devoid of life, creates a lonely atmosphere that is unnatural to our design.

Be sure to play with other living creatures daily so that you share in the needed energy exchange which will enhance your well-being.

Connection

Life thrives on connection. The interconnectedness of all life shows us everything we need to know. Nature is life. When we live naturally we stay connected to life-force energy that pulsates through every living organism on Earth. As we build our energy system through our sharing of this life-force energy, we feel good. Sharing promotes better health in everyone who participates.

Love is the sharing of positive energy with others. When we interact with love, we help to build the well-being of those with whom we connect. Endeavor to connect in love with all of life, and see how naturally healthy and happy you become.

Praise

Were you raised on praise for your natural instinct to act for the good of yourself and others? Or, did your caretakers use the fear and judgment method, scolding you for any perceived miss-step? Depending on the method used, you either developed a healthy self-esteem knowing of your innate goodness, or you feared judgment, hiding any perceived fault. The latter creates a withdrawn response due to feeling unsafe within one's own Self.

The remedy for this type of withdrawal from life is to realize the truth of your very Being. You are made in "the image of God", from the substance of God. Your Soul is connected to the awareness of God (ALL THAT IS) at all times. This knowing, logically, will empower you to take part in the co-creative process of life that you were designed to participate in.

Go deep within yourself to the place where all is well, your Soul. Allow yourself to be re-taught by this loving presence within you. Praise is all you will receive from your divinity.

Experiential Living

Life is designed in a way that needs to be experienced in order to be fully lived. How experiential is your life? Do you participate in adventures, or do you watch from the sidelines as others participate in the exciting experiences of life?

Do you share in the creative measures necessary for living, such as, building a home to live in, cultivating a garden for food or raising chickens for fresh eggs? Many people have lost these experiences by purchasing ready-made homes, and food from grocery stores.

Do you desire to take back more of the creative experience in living? Co-creation is our birthright. It fulfills needs deep within our psyche that nothing else can achieve. Become more active in the role of living, and heal this place within.

In Love

Are you a lover of life? Do you experience bliss while in Nature? Have you entered into the ecstasy of flowing with Earth's majestic rhythm? Nothing can compare with being "In Love" with life.

Meditating in Nature opens one's awareness of the magic of the cosmos. The interconnectedness of all life is a sacred understanding that brings peace within. Open your heart to this beauty. Feel the depth of your Soul. Allow yourself to experience your divinity, your oneness with all life. Fall "In Love" with life.

Well-being

We are designed to self-regulate. As long as we live in a natural environment without harmful toxins, our bodies will continually balance themselves to keep our health in-check. It is only by a dis-harmony with Nature that our bodies cannot compensate for the imbalance. Nature is always balancing itself, moment by moment. We too are made from Nature, and we can maintain our health by remaining in Nature.

The world designed by the ego-minds of humankind has taken us far off track from Nature. All sorts of dis-ease and illness seem to flourish daily due to this unnatural situation that we have brought ourselves into. It is time to reverse our ignorant decisions. We can no longer claim ignorance. We now know that Nature needs to be considered and worked with in order to promote the natural balance of life.

We have ventured far enough from our natural balanced state. We must act now to bring back Nature's balance. Our health and well-being count on it, as well as all of life on Earth.

Year Three

Year Three

Year Four

Creation

We live in a world that is supported by the foundational elements of life on Earth. This marvelous creation, Earth, is teeming with all that is necessary for living a happy, healthy and fulfilling life. Everything that pulsates with life-force energy expands and heals as connection and sharing occurs. The key is Nature, God's way.

There will come a time when people remain close to Nature to keep the balance for all future generations. We have reached the scare point in our unnatural way of living in this ego-mind world of man-made, artificial stuff. It is only a matter of time before those who hear the call within their Soul take appropriate actions to bring back Nature's balance.

God created from itself all that we see, taste, touch, hear, and smell. We co-create from the elements received from Nature. With imagination (the mental process of visioning what we desire to experience) we combine these natural elements to make what we want. As long as everything remains within the harmony of Nature, we can do no great damage. It is when we move out of this natural balance of Creation's way of thriving that we falter, setting up for ourselves imminent doom.

It is time to stop this insanity. As sane human beings, we must come back to Nature to reformulate the natural balance of the Universe.

Interpretation

There are so many views about life. From which viewpoint do you see your life experience? Does your belief system formulate success only from hard work? Or does the idea of success come from a deeper, more passionate place that fulfills the basic human need for love? Does your perspective come from interpreting life positively, where life is for you? Or, do you see life as a struggle with others acting as your enemy?

Become aware of your perspective. Beliefs have been handed down for generations, and it is these beliefs that keep the world of mankind in its current condition. To change life as we have known it, humanity must change the way they perceive it.

This is simple, though not always easy. Beliefs are not necessarily based on true reality. Rather, they are merely personal perceptions of reality. Whether interpreted as positive or negative, they can build up a person's character or crash them into victimhood. When you interpret a situation as something necessary for new growth then you will welcome the lessons learned. If you judge it as bad, you will feel weak like a victim.

Remember the story of the young man who obtained the new horse (thought of as good), that broke his leg (thought of as bad) so that he was unable to be drafted into the war (good), where all of the young men in his village were wiped out (bad), except for him? He could interpret this as a calling to help out his village in need; a noble purpose indeed.

Endeavor to use positive interpretation at all times. Life is truly for you. You just need to understand better how it works. Your Soul will always offer you what you need to grow and awaken to your divinity.

Congruence

There are multiple facets to every expression. Are you congruent throughout your very BEING? Do your thoughts, words and actions match consistently? Does your Soul's true desire make itself known to others by the way you live your life? Have you found yourself to be in alignment body, ego-mind and Soul?

You can use any formula that works best for you personally. Many find their way to unity within by first thinking, then speaking, followed by doing, until they become it. Others use the axiom: be, do, have. However you bring your life into congruence is yours to decide.

When all of YOU is aligned there is no greater power in the Universe. We suggest that you seek out your Soul's desire first (your reason for incarnating here on Earth), then bring your ego-mind into alignment, or agreement, with your Soul's purpose, and then take action with your body to match this true desire.

Becoming your Soul Self is the beginning of fulfilling your reason for being born. Congruence within and without is how life was intended to be expressed. Find your true desire and bring your life into congruence with your divine purpose. This will lead to true fulfillment.

YOU Have Created Your Circumstance

Yes, YOU have created all of your own circumstances. You will understand this Universal truth if you look at what you have accepted as your beliefs and follow the thread to the end result. Are you willing to look at this idea? If so, continue to read on.

We live in a fluid world designed by a multitude of belief systems. We call this the ego-mind world of illusion appearing as reality, when in actuality it is based upon nothing more than the thoughts and feelings of the masses that have been conditioned by fear.

Empowerment comes from looking beyond the 'veil'. This takes courage and determination. Your Soul has all that you need to break through this illusory world made by the human ego-mind. Be strong in your conviction to KNOW deep within just how transitory this ego-world of mankind is. It is not based upon the principles of life.

"Seek and you shall find," according to your determined conviction. Many masters have shown the way to Universal Truth. The only difference between them and you is determination and conviction. They sought until they knew. Nothing prevented them from breaking through the veil of illusion.

Nature shows us how life operates. Bring yourself back into balance with your natural expression and you will automatically better understand how life works. Empower yourself.

Free Yourself

"You will know the truth and the truth will set you free." Free from false beliefs. Free to express your divinity. Free to become your Soul Self.

How do you know what is truth for you? You feel exhilaration. You feel your connection to everything. You feel the ONENESS experience that the masters have been declaring for ages. You feel alive, well and generous.

The methods to reach this divine place within your very Being are many. Choose what feels right to you. Meditation (sitting in silence to hear and feel the wisdom of your Soul) is the most popular method, and yet, there are multitudes of ways to meditate. You can also experience your truth while walking alone in Nature connecting to Earth's rhythm, dancing euphorically while experiencing the interconnectedness with others, or while using your imagination to create a future event.

Knowing is experiential. Do not be afraid to experience life. Free yourself.

Worship

There are so many views about how human beings should worship. There are as many ideas as there are colors in the color spectrum. It would not make sense to limit what colors should be used in painting a landscape, would it? Neither does it make sense to limit how to worship.

Variety is God's gift. Life is filled with great diversity. Only human beings fight one another over the subject of worship. The animal and plant kingdoms are not as petty. What does this tell us about Nature? It tells us that there is no single way to live. Please take heed of this valuable information and make peace with each other.

Nutrition

What is your favorite fruit? Why? Is it the taste, texture, color, smell or food value? Do you feel energized after eating it? Does it satisfy your sweet-tooth? Is it a good source of fuel for your body? Is its ease and accessibility enough to constitute it as 'fast food?'

Nature creates the perfect food designed for our bodies. Organically grown grains, nuts, fruits and vegetables contain all of the necessary ingredients to sustain a healthy body. And, everyone has the ability to grow their own produce for their consumption. God has given us a bounty. It is up to us to do our part to feed ourselves wholesome, life-sustaining nutrition.

Natural Shelter

Nature provides the raw materials to create valuable shelter for ourselves. Animals in the wild are quite industrious with their homes. We too can build good, strong fortifications for our families using natural materials.

A lot of unnecessary pollution can be avoided if we were to utilize what Nature provides. Everything in Nature is designed to break-down, back into the ground, to be re-used as fuel for the soil. Man-made items do not feed the soil, but rather, they create toxins that destroy Nature's balance.

You can do your part to work with Nature's balance when building your family's shelter.

Future

How often do you spend time alone contemplating your future? Do you take an active role in designing your life? Do you make preparations for improving your circumstances? Are you learning new skills to assist you in your progress? And, do you enlist the help of qualified teachers to aide your learning process?

There is much you can do to improve your future, and the future of generations to come. It is in your hands to choose just how much you are willing to participate in. Life is a gift that we can enhance.

Meditate, contemplate, design and create your desired future.

Multidimensional

We are multidimensional beings. Our life here on planet Earth is only a fraction of who we are. As divine beings, we have the privilege to access our other dimensions at will. This, of course, takes skill and diligence. Also, having the assistance of a qualified teacher is very helpful, indeed.

And yet, it would do us little good if we have not first brought our earthly life into balance. It is similar to spending our time and resources on space travel when our earthly home needs our attention. What can you do today to bring your current circumstances into greater balance? Why not focus on that, until you complete it, before you endeavor to pull your attention away to non-earthly matters.

Resilience

You have a choice as to how you desire to live your life. It may not seem that way to you because of the ego-mind program that tells you that you are victim to the circumstances of this world, but truly, you can direct just how much of the 'poison' from disconnected hearts affects you, personally.

We will expound: your vibration will attract everything into your life, without exception. If you buy into the FEAR of the ego world you will suffer more than if you hold steadfast to the Universal Truth found in Nature, which is – "There is a time and a season for everything under the sun."

Nature is resilient. It will seek to balance itself at whatever cost. You are created by Nature, and your body will seek to balance itself wherever possible. Sometimes this balancing act looks like disease, but this is only a clue that you have gone too far off the 'norm' to recover naturally. Seek immediate help when you find yourself under this duress.

You can avoid many of the pitfalls of imbalance by remaining true to your natural state, which is in alignment with NATURE. Balance is a key factor to well-being. Choose to stay as close to Nature as you know how.

Natural Teachers

How often do you go outside into Nature? Do you connect with the animal kingdom regularly? Goats are as natural as life itself. There is not much that can take a goat out of its natural state. We recommend that you seek the company of goats often. They have much to teach you.

For instance: goats will seek shelter wherever possible from heavy storms, and yet, they can also endure hardship by forming a ring of protection by standing together. Elephants do this as well, but goats are more available to observe.

Also, goats can avoid starvation by accessing nutrition from the least nutritional sources. They have an aptitude for survival. They are not as finicky as other creatures, their will to survive outweighs their desire for comfort.

And, goats will work together for the good of the herd, as well as individually. They use the axiom; 'and/both' very well. They are excellent teachers for surviving in the most natural way possible.

Goodness

Life is filled with numerous challenges that can pull one off balance. The key is to remain flexible, open hearted and connected to Source. Faith in one's Soul can bridge the gap when difficulty arises. We are truly divine beings, which means that we can never be disconnected from God, ALL THAT IS.

Trusting in the goodness of life empowers our choices. When we perceive life as FOR us, we generate the proper energy to bring into our experience all that is necessary for our well-being. Continue to develop a strong positive attitude toward life and experience the desired results.

Joy is an elixir that uplifts every cell in your body. You can redesign your future for the better by taking the time necessary to enhance your faith in goodness. Everyone is doing the best that they can with the understanding that they hold. Improvement comes with greater understanding of Universal principles.

Healing Trauma

Everything can be healed, although not always cured. To cure is to bring back to the state before the ailment. To heal is to overcome in the face of difficulty. A car accident may leave you without all of your limbs. You can surely heal yourself to the point that you are able to live your life well without an arm or a leg.

Trauma can cripple you in more ways than one. Emotional health is usually the most difficult to heal. And yet, we say that it really can be the simplest. Acceptance is the first key. Once you accept what has occurred, you can then adjust to the new circumstances. Without acceptance there can be no true healing.

The second key is to grieve your loss. You will never be the same again. This is alright. Nothing stays the same.

And, third, keep moving forward with your desires. You know what you need in your life to feel fulfilled. Adjust yourself accordingly, but never give up your dreams. There are more ways than one to fulfill your passions. Search for the opportunities that will bring about your joyful expression.

Love is Natural

You know deep within that there is nothing but LOVE. Every creature expresses from the consciousness that they have formulated from all of the experiences in their life drama. Many have endured horrific circumstances due to the failure of the unnatural ego-mind world to understand Universal Truth; Love is natural.

It is a privilege and an honor to awaken beyond the physical senses and intellect of this ego-world. Your Soul stays tuned into the direct stream of Source at all times. This keeps you breathing. It is up to you, though, just how aware you can be of love's presence.

Open your heart to feel more deeply the interconnectedness of every living thing on Earth and in the Universe. Source energy is available to ALL. Choose to experience its flow.

Divine Ecstasy

How often do you experience ecstasy? This inner exhilaration is a sign of a deep connection to Source. Many Saints and Gurus have shared their experiences of bliss and ecstasy with the world. They have shown that it is possible to enter into the universal flow of love, life-force energy, available to all.

This divine energy of love washes over one's being in a way that clears out the cobwebs of false teachings of fear, judgment, condemnation and punishment.

Allow yourself to experience love's divine flow of rapture, and then share your new understandings with others. Help them to know just how possible true joy is for them to live and express.

Presence

Your presence is the culmination of all energies expressing through you. When you are flowing in love's natural rhythm, your presence is felt as warmth, safety and well-being. If you cut off this natural flow, you will be felt by others as cold, unsafe and lacking.

Why would you desire to stop your flow of love, life-force energy, and divinity? Can there ever truly be a reason to restrict God's light? If you believe 'love is the answer', then choose to flow. Melt away all that you hold in resentment. Clear away every repression. Stop suppressing your love.

"BE the change." Express your love openly, graciously. Make your loving presence felt far and wide.

Regenerative Sustainability

How deeply do you care for the well-being of planet Earth? Do your actions uphold your beliefs? Living by the wisdom teaching of 'Do no harm' is the beginning of properly caring for God's Creation. This will actually take care of the majority of the issues facing our planet.

Regenerative sustainability is the rest of the equation. Keeping the natural rhythmic cycle of life flowing will ensure that no creature become extinct. There is room for all of creation to co-habit together, as designed from the beginning.

We, as humans, must turn our harmful ways around NOW. It is up to each one of us to do our part to bring Earth back into its natural balance. What more can you do to make this happen? Do it.

Honest Appraisal

How honest are you with yourself about the activities that you participate in that cause harm to others? What about the harm you bring to yourself? Can Earth and all of her inhabitants continue to live with the increasing pollution that we create? Future generations are at risk. Extinction of wildlife is increasing daily. How can you help?

First, stop using man-made chemicals that rob Earth of her natural balance. Nature creates in a way that promotes life. Switch to using natural ingredients for all of your needs.

Second, recycle everything. Re-use all items that can be repurposed. This will slow down the landfill issues and the carbon footprint of consumerism.

Third, join others in their quest for the equanimity of all creatures. Every living being is sacred. All of creation is divine. We must choose to live with each other as brothers and sisters; human, animal, plant and spirit.

Wake yourself up. Act now. Become more involved in Earth's regeneration. Make a difference.

Restoration

Earth must be restored to her natural rhythm. It is mankind's obligation to right what has been wronged. Nature will balance itself when left alone. We must stop doing that which is harmful to allow for Earth to recover from the damage inflicted upon it.

We can also assist in Earth's repair by following more natural ways of living. We can green up the deserts by using techniques that mimic Nature. We can prevent further desertification by following natural principles.

Earth has been given into our care. It is up to each one of us to do our part to bring our home back into its natural balance. What role are you playing in Earth's restoration?

Caring for Animals

Human beings enjoy caring for their pets. They receive satisfaction from pampering their four-legged, feathered, and finned friends. The bonds created from this exchange are priceless.

All animals need our proper care. Even those in the wild are dependent on our keeping their habitat intact. There is so much that can be done to prevent the unnecessary extinction of any species. Do what you can today and every day to ensure the well-being of our amazing animal kingdom.

Food

Gardening is our privilege and our birthright. It is an honorable undertaking to provide food for ourselves and our loved ones. When we participate in the feeding of our family we gain the trust of those relying upon our provisions. It helps build security in this insecure ego-mind world.

God provides all that is necessary for us to thrive. Food grows abundantly in small plots of land. Even a balcony can grow enough fresh produce to take the edge off of the grocery bill. How much do you grow for yourself? Can you double this each year until you provide for most of your needs?

Community gardens are becoming quite popular for those who live in cities. Check out those that are in your area and connect with like-minded people to grow your food organically, God's way.

Compassionate Listening

Everyone desires to feel their innate innocence. There is a reason we behave in the manner that we do. Sometimes we do things that clearly are not in the best interest of ourselves or others. When these subconscious 'programs' take over, causing us to go against ourselves, we can create much harm. The key to avoiding this is in knowing our truth, our Soul's divinity.

Listen compassionately to your subconscious. Ask for clarity on why you behave certain ways and what you need in order to heal the held onto traumas. Become your own healer by working with all the differing aspects of your Being; body subconscious, ego-mind conscious and Soul super conscious.

With your conscious ego-mind as mediator, ask your body's subconscious to share with you what it needs to heal itself. Then, ask your Soul to do the healing by flushing your cells with divinity; Self LOVE. Practice this daily and you will become an integrated whole person, your Soul Self.

Transformation

There comes a time when we must transform our way of Being. When we see how ruthless greed can cause us to behave we know it is time for us to change. Godliness is not how much knowledge we have acquired. Rather, it is wisdom that brings our knowledge into action for the benefit of all. Creating a happy and healthy life then becomes more important to us than 'making a living.'

Count how much of your time is spent making money? How much of that would you still do if you were not paid? Creating a life of quality will bring your ratio closer to that which is fulfilling to your Soul. Choose to live each day to its fullest. Spend more time with Nature, family, friends and community. Transform your way of Being a little more each day to better create a life worth experiencing.

Natural Living

Have you been increasing your level of balance with Nature each day? Are you tuning your vibration to the rhythm of Nature, God's way? How often do you commune with the great outdoors? Can you make a conscious agreement to spend more time with Nature?

Even increasing your dosage in small increments will eventually bring you into a more relaxed state of Being. Natural living will improve your health and vitality. It will slow down the anxiety of the mind, allowing more clarity of thought. Nature's rhythm will assist you with your emotional well-being. Physical fitness is achieved through labors of love that bring a sense of positive pride for your great accomplishments that bring benefit to our planet and her inhabitants.

Earth was designed to be cared for naturally. We come from the Earth, as does everything organic. Choose to live naturally, in tune with Gaia. Decide now to adjust your way of life to better care for God's Creation.

Practical Spirituality

One must bring themselves into balance to be whole. The physical, or practical, is very important to maintain health. The spiritual is as important to sustain mental/emotional well-being. We need to balance both to gain wholeness.

With practical spirituality you will leave out no aspect of your Being; physical, emotional, mental, spiritual and energetic. The key to living a complete life is to care for all of your Self. Maintaining balance is a dance; listen within to the rhythm of your Soul and flow accordingly.

You will feel which steps to take, when to pause or change direction. Spend some time each day or week satisfying each of these aspects of you. Bring balance into your life and experience true fulfillment.

Allow

Do you allow your desires to manifest? How quickly do they appear? When you decide on what you wish to experience, does it come into your life within a few months? The faster your desires come into fruition, the more allowing you show yourself to be.

You can speed up the time frame with the conviction of your Soul. When what you desire is true to your Soul, you add the power of divinity. This will surely speed things up.

"When two or more are gathered" in like mind, the results increase in magnitude. A couple that is in true agreement can manifest their shared desires extremely well. Seek out those who share your passions.

Move forward towards your goal's completion, then choose another goal to fulfill. Allow the manifestation of your dreams.

Manifest

Allowing the Universe to bring you your desires is a most important step in the equation of manifestation. When you decide on what you want, there are certain motions that must take place to bring your desire into fruition. Allowing is a key factor.

Once you have permitted the fulfillment of the manifestation, it would do you well to express gratitude for its arrival. This true appreciation will keep the flow strong, so you can bring even more into your life. Practice being grateful daily and watch your ability to manifest improve with each successful fulfillment.

Mother

A mother's love is nourishing to all. Her fine attributes nurture the Soul. Her patience is priceless. As is her selfless service. She is known for her tenderness and compassion. A mother's protective nature ensures the well-being of her young, while her wisdom teachings prepare them for interdependence with community.

How can we show our appreciation for our mother's loving care? Emulation is the greatest praise. We show her how fond we are of her mothering by our loving attention. How fond are you of your mother?

Appreciation

When we show appreciation for our life, we build a strong foundation upon which to co-create our future. This foundation will support all that you desire to come into being. Keep your heart involved with every aspect of life. Choose wisely what you want to create and be grateful for its fulfillment.

A positive attitude towards life is more valuable than a paycheck. Make sure you enjoy your work. If you are only operating out of a sense of duty, your life will come short of true joy. Endeavor to live as fully as possible, fulfilling your Soul. This will naturally produce deep appreciation.

Anticipation

It is fascinating to us how often people tend to have a negative anticipation for their life circumstances. This shows us that most people do not understand their personal role in the development of their own life situation.

Worry is a negative anticipation. Fear is a negative anticipation. Doubt is also a negative anticipation.

Turn these into positive anticipation with the proper understanding of the principles that co-create your experience and you will gain confidence and certitude in your ability to create a more positive outcome for yourself.

Life is designed by YOU, along with your peers. Learn to a greater degree about your own role in your life's design. Take a greater responsibility for the thoughts you harbor and the feelings you feed. Change your perception from life being against you to life being for you. Recreate your life experience a little each day with affirmative ideas. Learn to anticipate exactly what you feel, and then learn to feel better.

Results

You are co-creating everything in your life experience by will or by default. Choose to be more active in your creations by taking the time necessary to DECIDE on exactly what you want to experience.

Use your imagination to design the life you desire. Use whatever materials that will keep you focused properly, such as vision boards, affirmations and pictures that capture the essence of what you desire to experience.

Communicate your desires to those who are in a position to either support you or encourage you on your journey. Make lists of the steps that need to be taken to bring your desire into manifestation. Then, take those steps.

Keep your focus until you reach your desired results. Celebrate your victories. And then, begin again.

Group Consciousness

As you develop your aptitude for creating what you desire, you will eventually want to use this formula to co-create with others of like mind. There is great power in numbers. Locate and invite others who share your passions to participate with you in co-creating the life that will bring you each true fulfillment. Share your mutual affinities. Enjoy the camaraderie.

Start with your basic desires; adequate shelter, clean air, pure water, organic food, positive companionship and supportive community. From here, add your own unique twists and draw to yourself those who share your aspirations.

Feel the power of group consciousness when everyone involved is on the same page. Utilize this group energy to its fullest. Co-create together.

Father

A father's strength of character gains the natural respect of his offspring. He need not use power over another to force obedience. Rather, his wise understanding of human nature gives him great influence. It is a blessing to all when a father teaches loving kindness, compassion and wisdom. His protection and provisions ensure the safety of his children.

How do we show our gratitude for our father's care? Honoring his wisdom and forgiving his ignorant ways can lead to a greater relationship. How grateful are you of your father?

Variety

How well do you enjoy the variety in life? Can you open yourself to appreciate more? Will you allow yourself to tolerate those who desire things differently than you? Can you live peacefully alongside people who operate from another perspective? Are you willing to accept cultural differences?

When we get down to the basics, there is not much difference between humans. The diversity comes in the extras. There is enough diversity for everyone to fulfill their own unique desires. Know this to be true: you can have what you want, while others co-create what they desire. There is enough for all.

True Joy

How often do you experience true joy? We would say – not enough! Joy is the universal elixir of life. Why are you denying yourself of this all-important formula? Open your heart to feel the joy of your Soul. This will bring passion, vitality and awareness into your life experience like nothing else.

Your Soul operates from its connection to Source, which is true joy. Become your Soul Self by fueling your passions, following your true desires and expressing your innate truth, which is joy.

Share Love

Every creature desires love. We are made from the building blocks of love. We emulate love. We thrive with love. There really is nothing other than love in the natural world. It is the unnatural expression of greed, selfishness and separation that cause the distortion in our way of life.

Bring yourself back into alignment with your truth, which is LOVE. Love is sharing. When we share, there is enough for all. Share your love with all of creation. Share your truth with all. Share your essence with God's Creation.

Design or Default?

How involved are you in deciding what type of life you are creating? Do you create by default? This is easy to do by doing nothing. Your life will evolve around your vibration. Your circumstances will be created from the frequency that you radiate.

Your ability to focus and participate in designing the future you desire is shown daily through the experiences that arrive in your life. How well do you prepare yourself to bring forth your desired results? Are you handing over your part to someone else to decide? If so, then why? Is this not your life to live? And, is this not each person's birthright to choose for themselves?

Are you ready to take the reins and do your part to choose wisely the design of your life? Allow your Soul to guide you and you will be sure to co-create that which is highest good for all life.

Now

We are accepting our involvement in life's happenings more and more. We are waking up again from the slumber of indifference. No longer can we allow lethargy to rob us of our power to change things. We must participate to bring about the changes necessary for our continued existence on Earth.

The time is NOW. It is up to each one of us to co-create with Spirit. Open your heart to hear the guidance of your Soul. Plan new ways of living that will create change. Expand your vibration to ever greater heights. Allow Nature to show you her principles for abundant living. Give yourself permission to affect life for the better.

Become the Change

Here we are in this age, ready to make the necessary shifts within ourselves that will change the current landslide of ecological destruction to our planet. How much are you doing to turn things around? Can you continue to do things that bring harm to the Earth? Will your heart allow you to knowingly bring ruin to our amazing home?

Ignorance is no excuse. There is enough information available for everyone to comprehend the urgency of our times. We must act now to affect change. Nature is God's way for harmonious living. How natural are you? Do you understand the language of life? Can you share your understanding of life's principles with others? Will you become the change so people can learn by example?

Magic

It is magical when our Soul shines through our heart. Like rays from the sun, our Soul radiates our love out from the center of our heart chakra. This magic illuminates our surroundings.

Falling in love has a very similar feel. When we fall in love we open our heart to connection with another. Inner peace washes over us. Positive excitement thrills us. Well-being surrounds us.

A parent's joyful connection with their child brings about this magic too. Fondness for our offspring enlivens us to our core. Fulfillment is experienced throughout our very Being.

Connecting with Nature awakens our Soul. We feel the presence of God, life, love. Divinity expresses through, and as us. We become magic.

We are made in the 'image of God.' Let us express our divine spark, our magic, for the benefit of all Creation. This is the 'change' we must become.

Natural Order

How do we create a better life for all inhabitants of planet Earth? It would make sense to live in harmony with the principles of Nature. There is no waste in the natural world. Everything recycles back to fertile soil to welcome new life.

We could learn a lot from observing and mimicking Nature; God's way. There would be no pollution or toxic waste build-up. Everything would flow through natural cycles. Regeneration is a key factor. Life promotes life. Even death promotes new life.

How can you choose today to live more in harmony with God's natural order?

Harmony

What does it mean to live in harmony with Nature? Life on Earth is a symphony among God's Creation. We are either adding to its beautiful sound or clashing out of sync, causing a disturbing noise that does not feel good.

We all vibrate sound. And, when we are happy, healthy and of genuine service we radiate tones of joy. This makes for a lovely symphony and we strengthen the true understanding of our co-creative force for good. We add to life's well-being.

When we fall short of this goodness, we create disharmony, illness and disease within ourselves, thereby affecting the entire planet. Judgment is the opposite of love.

Endeavor to raise your frequency to a higher vibration of love for all of Creation.

Believe

We are impressed with the amount of futurists there are in the world at this time. What do we mean by the phrase 'futuristic thinking', more specifically, 'holistic futuristic thinking?' To us there are two kinds of believers; Those who say, "I'll believe it when I see it." And, the others who declare, "I believe it, therefore I will see it." Which are you?

It is easy to be among the ones who wait for the creation of others to come into fruition. Yet, that is not how we as humans are designed. People have the innate ability and inner desire to co-create their life into what they want to experience. Boredom and depression set in when we are idle.

To be among those who co-create their world in a holistic manner, in tune with Nature, is the most fulfilling purpose a person can experience. Passion fuels their lives. True meaning is found. Life becomes an exciting adventure filled with mystical magic from their Soul.

Endeavor to become a positive participant in the design of your future, and the future of all Earth's inhabitants. Co-create what you desire by first believing in its future reality.

Positive Vibration

Everything is vibration. You can only attract what your vibration matches. Joy is almost a magical vibration, in that it attracts more good into your life than all other emotions. Judgment, on the other hand, will bring you dismay. What is your dominant emotion?

Endeavor to create more joy in your life. Look for ways to build up better feelings within you. Seek out those who share your passions. Meditate on bliss. Wake up with a smile to share with others. Enjoy your days more. Spend time with Nature.

Make little adjustments each day to co-create a better life. Catch yourself when you feel negativity, and turn your attitude around. You want to create from a positive vibration. Stay positive, look for solutions, ask for divine assistance, do no harm, and seek JOY.

Who Says?

Have you taken the time to examine your beliefs? Where do they come from? Did you adopt the ideas of your parents, school teachers, government, religion, peers, television, or maybe the internet? Why do you accept what others say?

If you meditate on your beliefs, you may find certain disharmonies within the ideas that you allow to germinate. Weed out those that stop you from expressing your joy. Replace judgment of others with self-discernment. Only accept the beliefs that bring you closer to your full expression as a natural human being.

Become aware of why you do what you do. Change the things that create havoc in your life. Steer yourself toward greater expressions of love, life, and joy.

Do Not Judge

Everyone is seeking to feel good. With all of the 'taboos' placed upon mankind, it can be challenging to find wholesome ways of expressing oneself. Why do you think this ego-mind world chooses to dictate what is 'right' or 'wrong'? Do you allow judgment to cloud your thinking?

In the Jewish and Christian scriptures it is written, "Do not judge." What part of that phrase do you not understand? Judgment closes the heart, the seat of the Soul, one's very own divinity. One must keep their heart open with love and compassion in order to be more God-like. How are you doing with this?

Can you open your heart more right now to bring through a greater expression of love for humanity? Are you willing to accept more diversity in your experience? Can you connect deeply to another through a Soul to Soul connection? Try it, you may find it very appealing.

Make Better Choices

"The powers that be" are human. All decisions are made by human beings. There is no authority in the sky that dictates how you are to live. There is, however, Universal Law. This law is based on natural principles of life.

You can choose to live in harmony with Nature, or not. It is your choice. Consequences occur naturally by every action we take. We must take full responsibility for our own choices. We cannot blame God, the Universe, the devil, or whatever else we put a label to our issues. It is human consciousness that co-creates the world we live in.

Become more active in your role as a co-creator. Make better choices for yourself that support the natural order of life on Earth. Tune-in to your Soul's guidance. For, it will guide you on how to be more harmonious with Universal Law.

Heart Center

Amongst the chaos of conflicting belief systems there is always peace within one's Soul. Stay in your center at all times. This is actually easier than it sounds. No one can take you away from your truth. Tides will rise and fall, but your center remains untouched. It is your safe haven.

In your heart center is the control panel for your consciousness. Your chakra system is interconnected. Make all of your decisions from this central station and see for yourself just how simple life becomes. You will have the clarity you need when you consult with your Soul. Allow your higher Being to guide you through the chaotic ego-mind world. It will not fail you.

Year Five

Open Heart

Now is all there is, always. Stay centered in the NOW by remaining in your heart. From this perspective you can see the true reality that love is all there is. When you are not feeling love, it is YOU that has restricted the natural flow.

Wisdom comes forth from your Soul. True understanding and compassion flow, like water down a stream. Be sure to not dam it up with judgment. Conviction for one's well-being will ensure that you keep your heart open at all times. To close one's heart is to shut down one's truth.

From the kindness of your Soul, share your wisdom with others. Those with open hearts will resonate with true wisdom. Highest good prevails in open-hearted people.

Open the Flow

Joy releases tension. Stress is caused by disconnecting from Source. Plug back into ALL THAT IS. Keep your energy flowing with the Universe at all times. Do not restrict life-force energy for any reason.

Ego-mind 'programs' that say you should deny yourself in order to be deemed worthy are falsehoods that actually cut you off from God. Nothing prevents life more than denial. Do not deny life, love, pleasure or joy.

Open the flow more each day and feel yourself building in strength, happiness and well-being.

Body Temple

Allow your body to speak your needs. Listen to how you feel. Find ways to feel better. Feed your body temple nourishing food. Hydrate with clean water. Breathe deeply to fill your lungs with fresh air. Soak in the Sun's rays a little each day. Touch the Earth at least once a day. Gaze at the stars each night.

Become more in-tune with Nature. Bring your rhythm into harmony with Mother Nature. Keep your heart open. Nature has all of the ingredients we need to live well. Give yourself much needed breaks from the man-made world.

Decrease the stress on your body by slowing down to the natural rhythm of life.

Simple Living

Those who have chosen to live more simply have found an increase in their well-being. There is a very good reason for this. The fast-paced ego-mind world can keep you off balance, causing stress induced illness. Simplicity helps to bring you back into the natural flow of life.

Many indigenous cultures have found the wisdom of living close to Nature. They put their emphasis on the well-being of the tribe. Children are treated as important contributors to the continuation of their culture. They are taught from an early age how to sustain a healthy life.

Re-train yourself to put the well-being of you and others as a priority. Well-being includes all aspects of life; physical, mental, emotional, spiritual and energetic. Live more simply.

Thought Vibration

How often do you meditate? Have you made this important spiritual activity a priority in your life? Everything begins with a thought vibration. Meditation slows down the ego-mind thoughts that race past you, so you can focus more clearly on what you desire to co-create for your life experience.

If you do not take the time to build your life the way you want it, in your imagination, you cannot expect to experience your desires. Spend more time participating in the preparation of your life course. Do not leave it to be designed by default. You will not be as happy with the results.

You are a co-creator. Meditate on what you desire to create.

Self-Aware

How does one go about designing a good life? First, get to know yourself; what you like, what feels good, what inspires you, what ignites your passion for living, etc. When you know more about yourself, that which is not imprinted upon you by others, then you can begin your life's design.

Finding out who you are begins the journey. Next, follow your instincts, gut feelings, intuition, etc. Become more aware of how you feel. Is what you are doing expanding your heart, or do you feel the contraction of your love?

Finally, we suggest that you accept that which you have already co-created (your past and present), and redesign your life experience from there. This way you are gradually and continually making adjustments and refinements in a manner that is easier to maintain.

Of course, if you are a daring type that needs excitement in your life, you can make drastic changes in your way of being, feeling the shifts taking place rapidly. Those who enjoy this type of adventure are more drawn to spirituality when it is exciting.

Choose what is right for you. Only a Self-Aware person can know how to design a life they would enjoy. Become Self-Aware.

Open Mind

Fun can include many perspectives. It is relative to the individual. By accepting all perspectives, and discerning for yourself that which resonates with you, you are more likely to enjoy life. Remember that ALL IS GOD. There are only differing degrees. Keep an open mind when viewing another person's consciousness (their lifestyle).

Do the same for yourself when you notice things in your life that you would like to change. Be gradual about it. Be kind to yourself while you are making the shifts. Keep your focus on that which you desire to manifest. Be patient with yourself. All is well.

Spiritual Guidance

How do WE share our wisdom with people? As Spirit, WE choose many avenues. WE enjoy speaking with those who have ears to listen. WE like to share through visions, the complete download experienced like a waking dream, full of the richness of a vivid imagination. WE nudge when fear causes the person to hold back.

How do you receive spiritual guidance? Does instinct grip you? Do you hear words? Can you see pictures, movies, or even experience a lucid dream? Do you sense, or smell, a change coming? Can you taste victory? These are the inner five senses, or as some call them; the sixth sense.

Explore your intuition. Open your mind to new experiences. Expand your heart to include more joy. Soak in the invigorating energy of Nature. Relax and enjoy the simple pleasure of being alive.

Divine Being

Open to the energy of life. Allow it to pulsate throughout your very Being. Remove thoughts, ideas and beliefs that limit the amount of life-force energy that flows through you. Become the divine human being that you were designed to be naturally. Accept your divinity.

See through the eyes of love. Hear with your inner ears of discernment. Intuit and sense the true fragrance of what's in the air through your Soul's knowing. Taste the full experience of your vivid imagination. Feel deep within the texture of emotion. Utilize all of your inner spiritual and outer physical senses. Use all of you to live life.

Captivating

Life is meant to be captivating. Humans love the thrill of excitement. We were designed to excel. Stop holding yourself back. Express fully your natural Self. Do not conform to mediocrity. Bust through the multiple levels of resistance to being divine. Be God.

Can you accept this idea? If you are struggling, ask within why? If you feel you are not capable yet, stretch further. Only YOU can prevent yourself from expressing your true divinity.

Compare yourself to no one. You can only decide for yourself what is right for you. Rely upon your own counsel. Feel into the rightness of your decisions. Act upon that which awakens more life, love and divinity.

Your Well-being

People truly want to feel good. Well-being is measured by the amount of physical health, emotional vibrancy, mental clarity, spiritual ecstasy and social connections. How is your well-being?

Do you need more rest or exertion? Are you happy with the life you have created or do you feel overwhelmed, depressed or anxious? Can you think clearly, focus and concentrate or is your thought process mottled and dim? Do you experience inner peace and bliss or are you feeling a lack of fulfillment? Do you have a close friend, family member or lover to keep you socially connected?

Increase your well-being daily. It is simple; Give yourself what you need and avoid that which robs you of your joy.

Life is Good

Do you feel the beauty of life-force energy pulsating through your very Being? This exhilarating experience is what keeps your body in good health, your emotions freely flowing and your mind clear. When you restrict this flow you may feel weak, depressed and confused.

Life is meant to be enjoyed. Our bodies are designed to regenerate. Our emotions are more positive when we flow. And, our thinking process becomes crisp and clear. How are you feeling?

Spend time every day opening to the flow of life-force energy. Move your body in Nature. Feel the aliveness of Spirit. Express your fullness. Lift your emotional well-being with positive input. Relax into the knowing that life is good.

Opportunity

When you are hungry you make yourself a meal. When you are lonely you seek out friendship. When you are tired you find a resting place. And, when you feel upset or depressed you must change your attitude to a more positive outlook in order to feel better.

You have more control over your life than you give yourself credit. You can shift your mood in a moment. You can earn money to pay your bills by offering your skills to someone in need. There are countless opportunities available to you at all times.

Become more aware of your ability to co-create a better life. Ponder on that which you can do to improve your circumstances. Do not wait for someone else to offer it to you, instead, seek out that which you need to care for your needs.

Better yet, plan how you can fulfill your desires. Trust that you are in charge of your personal life experience. Do your part.

God's Blessings

How many times in your life have you felt God's Blessing? As many as you were willing to experience. Yes, that is accurate. God IS Blessing, period. God is life. God is everything, in differing degrees. How much of God's goodness are you willing to experience? How much of God are you willing to express?

Why would you ever choose to restrict the flow of God's beautiful, life-giving energy of LOVE? Have you been misinformed about God's Creation? Has your mind been bent to believe in anything other than the true power of God's love? Shake yourself awake, now.

Nothing can exist apart from God. So, the more you open to real love, the current of life, the more you will experience God's ever-present Blessings.

Joyful Expression

When was the last time you felt good all the way through your very bones? What were you doing at the time? Can you see the divinity in it? Can you taste the sweetness of life in it? Can you feel the magic in it? Can you smell the clarity you attained? Can you hear your Soul's whisper? Can you touch God now?

Restricting one's joyful expression is like clamping a hose, preventing life-giving water from reaching its thirsty party. God does not restrict life. Only those separated from truth ever restrict the goodness of life's expression. Open your heart and mind to the ever flowing goodness of life's nourishing expression of JOY.

Move On

How can you shift your awareness from what is bothering you to that which would bring about relief? Try to shorten the time you need to figure out what is causing you distress. Once you realize that you are feeling less than optimal seek to find the antidote.

For instance, when you feel physical pain in your body, locate the issue and remove the cause, such as, finding and removing a pebble from your shoe. If the problem is chronic, then it is time to look deeper into the cause, which may be emotional or environmental. Seek out that which would bring a permanent relief, like expressing pent up emotional trauma, or removing the toxins in the environment.

Once you have discovered the underlying issue and removed that which was causing you anguish, then you can replace the old feelings of discomfort with more appropriate feelings of gratitude for the problem solved. Do not get hung up on the uncomfortable feelings. And do not keep the old emotions current by retelling your story over and over. Try to move on, instead.

This can be difficult. Many people like to share their tough stories with others. This does not serve a positive purpose, unless you are sharing from a place of strength in order to assist someone else to overcome the same issue.

Be careful to keep yourself current and positive. You do not want to recreate the difficulty by keeping it in your thoughts. Move forward into your positive co-creative ventures. Leave the past behind you.

Improve Your Life

We all desire to feel good. There are multiple ways to experience good feelings, positive adventures and healthy pleasure. Seek out that which brings a smile to your mouth. Act upon those things that delight you, even tickle you deep inside. Follow your enthusiastic excitement. Create a life that you like living.

Since most of your time is experienced with yourself, it would be wise to become someone whom you enjoy hanging out with. Do you lift your own spirits? Do you engage yourself in activities that delight you? Do you seek positive outlets to express your creativity?

Take the time necessary to determine what you can do to improve your life. Act upon that which comes to you from deep inside. Motivate yourself to desire a healthier lifestyle. Bless your life's future. Start now, even if it is only small steps at first. As you gain confidence, you will be able to increase your part in the co-creation of your life experience.

Start Again

Are you ready to live in your Soul's full expression? Why not? What do you consider is unworthy of your Soul's expression? Stop it. Shift your awareness to that which is your truth, your divinity. When you fall short, start again. You may have to start again hundreds of times a day. That is ok. Eventually you will conquer your negativity, through diligent persistence.

The sooner you begin again, the sooner you will experience your new creation, your new life. Do not become discouraged by the amount of times you need to start over. Learn to laugh at the silliness of your ego's stuckness. You can prevail. Your Soul's divinity is more powerful than your ego-mind's negative programming.

It is diligent action that brings about change. Is it time for a change in your life?

Life's Diversity

There are so many ways to express life. Why limit any of them? Some enjoy a more peaceful existence. Others prefer excitement. You may like hard physical work. Your neighbor may choose to use their intellect over physicality. Any way you choose to express your desired way of living is yours to choose. We suggest that you choose what brings you joy.

We also encourage you to accept another's way of life for them. Endeavor to see through their eyes to find the joy they experience with their personal choices. Even if they choose suffering, it is still their choice. All you can do is live your own example and invite them to join you if they choose. And, if they don't, then leave them be in their own choosing.

There is no single way to live properly. Enjoy the diversity of life.

Right to Choose

How can you appreciate the right for each person to choose for them how they prefer to live? You can start by appreciating your own right to choose for you. When you do something, you open the door for others to do likewise. Begin with yourself.

Have you taken the time to consider how you really want to experience your life? Are you living your ideal now? If so, well done. If not, then why not? Whose life are you living? Your parents', your educators', your mate's or maybe a favorite relative's? Why not live your own life?

You were born to live your own life. Take the time to figure out how you wish to live it to the fullest. Seek out people who share your passions. Find ways to accelerate your choice. Become attentive to the yearnings of your Soul.

Wisdom is Experiential

Allow yourself to learn wisdom through whatever means you choose. You can learn many things by observing the efforts of others, but true wisdom is experiential. Do not be afraid to learn for yourself firsthand. Just try to learn quickly, with as little harm done as possible. There is no need to drag out any unpleasant experience. Life is too short for that.

Keep an open mind and open heart. See for yourself what feels right to you. Change the things that do not bring joy or fulfillment. Adjust your circumstance to fit your idea for a life that you desire. Change your perception on things that do not work. Seek out those who share your choices. Live for the enjoyment of living. Bring joy to others. Live fully.

Stay Connected

We appreciate people who smile or say hello. It helps us feel connected to the human race. Even a wave from afar can light us from within.

How often do you greet a stranger passing by? Do you wave to your neighbors? Have you met everyone on your block? Do you keep in touch with friends and family? How connected are you?

How often do you write a letter, make a phone call or connect with those special ones in your life? Endeavor to make time for people. Staying connected is good for the Soul.

Natural Beauty

How often do we see beauty in Nature; raw, unadulterated, glorious beauty?

Our Soul thrives on natural beauty. We feel invigorated by the warmth of the sun, calmed by the puffy white clouds in the spacious blue sky, and held close to God with the sound of a babbling brook. Nature is our cure for city stress.

Seek out Nature often. Rejuvenate your body daily with fresh air and exercise. Walk among God's Creation to uplift your Spirit. Free yourself in the natural beauty and freedom of Nature.

Begin with YOU

Would you like to see a world filled with compassionate people who truly care about the well-being of others, including every living being in existence? Yes? Then it must begin with YOU.

When you have mastered real love, you will naturally draw to yourself more loving people. When you have done all you can to help improve your own caring, you will bring to yourself others who care.

As you gather to yourself those who desire to preserve life, in all its forms, you will create a community of compassionate and caring people who are not afraid to uphold Nature's balance. This is necessary for the continuance of life.

Start with yourself, and create the space where others of like mind can join you. Build your group strong and take action where you feel it would be helpful to the continuation of life and love. No step is too small.

Open Your Heart

Where will you find compassion within yourself? It is the energy of the heart. You must open your heart to feel and express compassion. It is tied to empathy, fellow feeling and respect for the rights of others to choose for themselves how to live their own lives.

We are each born with free will to choose how we want to experience life. We are born with an innate goodness and natural caring for others. It is twisted beliefs handed down from former generations that cause us to close our heartfelt compassion for people and animals.

We must re-open our hearts to love. We can accomplish this because it is our true nature. Recall a time when you felt such depth of love for someone, even an animal. Build your energy back with this fond memory, until you experience it as if it were yesterday. Continue building your heart muscles until you cannot fathom ever causing harm to another.

Compassion will change the world.

Re-Awaken Your Humanity

Where has our humanity gone? As greed takes over our world, it brings destruction to all life on our planet. Are we so short-sighted that we do not see the harm being done in the name of progress? How can harming life on Earth even be considered at all?

We need a new world view; One that takes into consideration the Earth's ecological well-being. After all, this is our home. It is up to us to care for Earth properly. We must unite with those of like mind, in order to create the necessary changes.

Take up your stance, and back it with positive action. Get involved wherever you feel motivated. Bring about change by re-awakening your humanity.

Family Unit

Have you noticed how often a person checks the time? With so many things vying for our attention in life, it does one well to decipher that which is truly important. Family is one of those important things. Relationships are strengthened with attention.

Caring for the family unit of husband and wife, and which may also include small children living at home, is the vital key to happiness. All other family relations can be considered as extended family, whose relationships are of a less crucial nature. Take care of your family unit first and foremost. All else will then fall into place.

Work, hobbies, friends, etc. are better placed appropriately around the health of the family unit. The well-being of your family is essential to experiencing a successful life. Work is a means to provide for this unit. Hobbies create opportunities to express one's self, and may be shared with the family. And, true friends can be helpful in the caring of the family.

Remember to put your family unit in top priority.

Soul Self

Wherever you are in the stages of your life, YOU are your greatest responsibility. When you have taken the time to become your highest potential, you then have more to offer to others. So, take the time to uncover your blueprint, your purpose, your Soul's reason for incarnating.

Once you know who you are, you will naturally attract to yourself others of like-mind. Building momentum becomes easy, because of the trajectory you create with Self-awareness. Call to you everyone and everything that will assist you in your Soul's expression.

Become your true Self, your Soul Self.

Nature's Example

Earth is home for so many creatures. We all share this life-sustaining planet. May we be considerate of the well-being of all Creation, excluding no living being?

Can you deepen your caring for others? Will you look out for the well-being of animals, insects and plants? Are you willing to promote the health of planet Earth, by insisting on creating pure air, water, and soil?

How much do you do to prevent harm, and promote well-being? Nature is a living example of how to keep balance. It is God's way. Learn from Nature.

God IS

GOD is a big word. We would say that there is no one way to describe God. Therefore, every description is accurate. If you believe that God is ALL THAT IS, there is nothing that is not God.

How on Earth can there be so much fighting over God, who is omnipresent, omnipotent, omni-everything? It just does not make sense.

God is love. Love encompasses all. God is life. Life sustains life. Simply put, God IS.

Experience Happiness

Happiness has been sought after for many years. Yet, it is nowhere to be found in any form. It is formless. You cannot find it, you can only feel it. It is an experience to be had in the moment.

Rather than chasing that which is elusive, why not just allow the experience? Feel the joy of being alive. Open your heart to cheerfulness. Delight in the simple pleasures of Nature.

Find ways to allow more happiness in your life.

Reverence

How can we show more reverence for life? In what ways can we operate man-made systems with Nature as our guide? Where will we find true cooperation among people? Who among us are showing positive protection and care for our home, the Earth? When will heart centered actions to maintain the balance of Nature become the norm? Why do we feel the need to desecrate our planet for profit?

Will you take the time to investigate natural solutions and implement them in your own daily life? This is the surest way to bring about positive change. Begin at home. Then, spread your love out from there to every aspect of living.

Become reverent toward God's natural ways. Revere Nature, our Creator's design.

Organic Systems

Nature operates all systems in an organic way. Somehow, mankind has deemed it inferior. How can we humans even conceive of the thought that God got it wrong? Clearly, it is mankind's interference with God's way that has caused the imbalance to Nature's organic systems.

When will we wake up to the fact that our ego-mind ways are not as efficient as our Creator's? It is time to get back to NATURE and allow our precious Earth the time to recuperate. Only then will we be able to share Earth with our great-grandchildren.

Interdependent Sharing

As natural as sharing a blanket with a loved one during a snow storm, we do well to share our Soul too. Our Soul knows the interdependence of life. We are designed to share with each other.

A single person seeks to share love with a partner. A couple may naturally seek to share their love with offspring. Families look to community to share land, water, food, etc. And, communities depend upon global humanity to keep Earth's balance.

Begin seeing your interdependent need of others, including plants and wildlife. Stretch yourself to appreciate that nobody can live independent of other living organisms. We need each other, not only to survive, but to thrive.

True Sharing

"LOVE is a many-splendored thing." This song reveals "a reason to be living." What is your reason for living?

Do you focus on getting, giving, or sharing? There is a difference between each of these avenues. Getting focuses on oneself, primarily the ego-mind. Giving focuses on the other, sometimes at your own peril. Sharing utilizes both receiving and giving simultaneously.

You can go out of balance in your getting and/or giving at the detriment of others or yourself. While sharing keeps the equilibrium intact; a win-win solution.

Endeavor to share real love with each and every being on Earth. You cannot go wrong with true sharing.

Love Completely

"How do I love thee? Let me count the ways." Do you love to the depth and breadth and height your Soul can reach? What stops you short? God's love is everlasting. Is yours?

Judgment prevents one from truly loving. That is why we are admonished, "Do not judge." And, yet people continue to judge one another so harshly that love is shaky.

How do you propose to change this in your own life? Will you raise your consciousness to the point of non-attachment? When your attachment to your own belief becomes more important than the person you disagree with, your judgment becomes dangerous.

Allow LOVE to pervade all situations, without exception. Then, you can say that you love completely.

Recharge

There are so many ways to experience life. Why limit yourself? Choose what brings you joy, excites your Soul and brings you closer to your Soul's expression.

Where do you receive your truest enjoyment? What activities delight you? Who lifts your spirits?

Be sure to spend time alone, communing with your Soul, as well as with others. Time alone will recharge your 'batteries.' This will give you more energy to share with other people when you meet up with them again.

We all need to keep ourselves fully charged, in order to bring true value to any get-together. Otherwise, we may bring people down with our weak energy. This can be avoided by wise decisions that keep us in the flow.

Remember that every interaction is a sacred one. Become a blessing to all.

Become a Gift to the World

How many ideas do you find titillating? Where do you experience deep pleasure? Some people experience bliss while in Nature. Others find their delight in family sharing. Whatever the avenue, utilize what works for you.

The more joy you experience, the more you have to offer others. It is not selfish to seek out that which builds you up. You can only give what you yourself receive. So, endeavor to receive more. Open your life to experience all that you can. Become a gift to the world.

Good Vibes

Whenever you experience something, your energy radiates from you, and therefore affects everyone around you. Knowing this may cause you to be more careful in your dealings. Endeavor to choose experiences that will bring joy to you, and thereby others.

Being mindful is an act of kindness. We say, "Excuse Nothing." Because everything matters. All life is affected by the vibrations that we emanate. Keep yourself in good vibes.

Fairies

We are inclined to share with you the many wonders of the Spirit world. You may have heard of Fairies, yes? We delight in their gaiety. They bring much to the table, so to speak.

Have you had your own experience with them? You probably have, without knowing. Especially, if you have spent time alone in a natural setting far from the hustle and bustle of the ego-mind world.

They keep themselves deep in the woods, jungles and anywhere uninhabited by people. Seek them out, gently. You will need to resonate love of Nature to call them to you. For, they are Nature's ambassadors.

Their gentleness is reviving. They will fill you with 'Fairy Dust' if you are open enough. The bliss that this brings will keep you coming back for more. And, you will be inclined to save the forests, their home.

Reach out to all the Spirits of this world and share in the blessings that they offer. Please bless them in return.

Loving Flow

Love is life. The more you love, the more life-force energy flows through your very Being. You are in command of your life and what you choose to fill yourself with – joy or angst. Joy opens the passageways, while angst causes constriction. Which would you rather experience?

Judgement is one of the greatest detriments to loving flow. It binds you up and blocks life-force energy. You would do well to erase your judgments. They are only ideas that you have adopted and formed belief systems around. You can dissolve their hold on you by feeling love for all living Beings.

Remember, God loves everyone.

Fellow Comrades

Here we are, as a human race, endeavoring to create a way of life that is sustainable for generations to come. We are finding that the closer we work with Nature, the better the plans. Life is designed to be regenerative and restorative. There are cycles and seasons. Even the aging process is slow enough to work around, so that we can experience and express our true desires if we are diligent and persistent.

How many things have you accomplished on your 'bucket list?' Are you making plans now to complete everything you desire? Do you need the assistance of others in community? How can you make your needs known to those who share in like-mindedness?

Gather to yourselves all whom would bring your plans into reality. Call forth your fellow comrades and co-create the experience together that suits everyone's needs.

Are You A Mystic?

Where have all the mystics gone? Are you one in hiding? Do you need to be awakened? Ask your Soul to guide you as you live your life. Bring into greater awareness your Soul's purpose for incarnating at this time. What are you to accomplish? Who are you to assist? Where are your people of like-mind?

As you become clearer in your knowing, act upon the guidance. Look for the coincidences, serendipity and answers to prayers. Your Soul is fast at work to bring you closer to your goals. Align your ego-mind with the direction of Spirit and let the games begin. Life is meant to be fun.

Healthy Designs

We live in a time of great inventions. People are able to bring into fruition the thoughts on their minds. Manifesting has become easy, in this way. And yet, not all designs are healthy. It would be more productive to create something that has no harmful effects on the well-being of living organisms.

Endeavor to find new ways of living that are more in accord with Nature. Seek to rebuild the Earth. Choose wisdom over greed, love over profit, and joy over success. You will enjoy your life more when you live in harmony with Nature.

Procrastination

How many times have you said to yourself, "Maybe tomorrow I'll do that" or "Maybe next year will work out for me to complete that project"? And, how much of that do you actually accomplish?

Is it due to procrastination that it doesn't get done, or do you change your mind on what you want? If it is the latter, then you will feel relief. If it is due to procrastination, then you may feel tension until the task is completed. Become stress free by taking action on what you desire, and keep moving forward in your life.

Soul Knowing

There are so many things in this Universe that you could not know them intimately through your ego-mind consciousness. It is through your Soul that you know them, because your Soul IS them; Connected with everything/All That Is/Source.

Become the full expression of your Soul. Dissolve the ego-mind programs that keep you in fear and lack. Expand your awareness to include everything possible for the betterment of this world.

Pure Being

Every once in a while you see through the veil of illusion into the purity of Spirit. This place of pure Being is where the Soul resides. Endeavor to connect there often. Find your center, the 'eye of the storm,' and focus your attention on your Soul's purpose.

Bring more clarity through the confusion of the mental world. Experience your divine knowing that love is truly the answer to every question. Remain in balance with Self-love and love for others.

Build your strength by aligning your ego with the guidance of your Soul. Bless all life.

Heal Yourself

There are more ways to heal than there are to comprehend. Utilize every avenue available to bring back wholeness within yourself. Find the joy in life. Seek out true loving connection with other heart-centered people. Allow Nature to soothe your Spirit. Find God in all things.

Become a source of inspiration for others. Give the gift of love's vibrational healing power. And, express your Soul's knowing.

True Reality

Open your heart to the Universe. Allow all the energy of Spirit to infuse you with joy. Give yourself the time to commune with your Soul each and every day. Explode with the passion and enthusiasm of your life purpose.

Remember who you really are. This deep knowing will keep you serene, even amongst the turmoil of this ego-mind world. Escape from the grasp of fearful thought, and enjoy the bliss of God's true reality which is LOVE.

Universal Light

Spirit is the place between thoughts and matter. It is also thoughts and matter. Spirit is life. Spirit is God. It is everything and nothing.

When you are about to make a decision in life, ask Spirit to show you the proper direction to take that will be highest good for all. When you do this, you will be infused with love and your desire will be to create well-being for the entire planet and all who live here.

Practice the art of communing with Spirit on a daily basis. Be guided by the light of the Universe.

Soul Sovereignty

The vision for Earth at this time is to recover Soul Sovereignty. When all work together as ONE, like the body of God, we shall know peace.

There is great diversity in God. The ego-mind judgments, rules and regulations create a false sense of smallness in the world. Let go of needing things to be a certain way. Instead, ask within for the highest and best way. Love will answer.

Good Company

Where has your enthusiasm for life taken you? What brings out the best in you? Who speaks the language of your Soul? Find the answers to these questions and follow them whole-heartedly.

Keep yourself in good company. Be resourceful in all your dealings so that you can spend more time in bliss. Create opportunities to share in friendship with other heart-centered people. Keep your spirits up.

Afterword
The Ancient Ones

We hope that our love for humanity shows through in our messages. We are thrilled to participate with you in co-creating a world system that encourages true Self-expression, passion in purpose, camaraderie among fellow humans, equivalence with all life forms, harmony with Nature, Divinity of the Soul, conscious participation as co-creators, and understanding of the monumental role of each individual's affect within the collective.

Our goal is to inspire and awaken your inner knowing of these wisdom teachings. Open your mind to the logic, your heart to the understanding, your instinct to the feeling, and your intuition to the knowing. It is ALL WITHIN YOU. And, it is all attainable.

This is the collection of five years of messages put into book form. We plan on continuing this series with each year to come. Thank you for participating with us in this New Era of Divinity.

Offerings to Enrich Your Life at Soul Self Living

Our purpose is to assist humanity to awaken their deep inner knowing from within their Souls, allowing perceptual changes to broaden their acceptance of individual creativity and value, combining with the collective consciousness of the whole to bring about cooperation, harmony and unity for the highest opportunity of all.

It is our desire to be of service in providing this transformative material. We have designed the Soul Self Living website and our books to assist individuals to awaken at their own pace, as their inner process unfolds. We are honored to share in this sacred connection of Souls awakening to their true divinity. May we all come to live a Soul Self life, accepting each individual as a brother or sister, working in unity to bring forth peace, wisdom and love.

We are also honored to deliver the illuminating messages channeled through Stacey by "The Ancient Ones". Their wisdom and guidance is a blessing for all of humanity. We hope their message spreads far and wide.

~ Jack and Stacey Stephens

Find all of the following offerings at SoulSelfLiving.com

Online Course –Awaken Your Soul

In this self-paced online course you can learn how to create more balance, harmony, and well-being in your life. Well-being encompasses every area of your life: physical, emotional, mental, spiritual, energetic, relational, financial, environmental, etc.

The Ancient wisdom made current in this course can help you shift into deeper intimacy with your Soul. As you become best friends with this Divine aspect of yourself, you can improve your own well-being and better assist those you love.

Awaken Your Soul is the complete collection of over 400 messages/lessons from The Ancient Ones channeled over the course of 10 years by Stacey Stephens.

Spiritual Coaching

Imagine…

- Having an unlimited supply of energy
- Enjoying physical, mental, and emotional health
- Experiencing the fulfillment of your deepest desires
- Loving the richness and closeness of your relationships
- Feeling invigorated and inspired by your work
- Expressing yourself with clarity and confidence
- Making a significant difference in the lives of others
- Being truly happy and fulfilled

Over the past 25 years Jack Stephens has helped hundreds of people like you shift their perception and create the best versions of their lives.

Channeled Vibrational Healing Intensives

Whether you are facing a physical illness or injury, suffering from emotional trauma, seeking mental clarity, or desiring energetic or spiritual support for your well-being, you don't need to struggle on your own any more.

Stacey Stephens offers an energy healing service called a Channeled Vibrational Healing Intensive in which The Ancient Ones work through her to perform healings.

Further Reading

The Complete *Messages from The Ancient Ones* Series

These books, channeled through Stacey Stephens, contain Universal wisdom for the transformation of individual and collective consciousness. We are so pleased to share them with you now, in this published collection of public communications from The Ancient Ones. Simple, yet profound, each message touches the hearts and Souls of every reader willing to experience more of their divine nature. They are Amazon.com Top 10 Bestsellers.

Express As YOU: Celebrate Your Uniqueness

"This book is a very personal one, in that I wrote it for myself, for my own evolutionary process. It is quite dense, which is why it is not very long, because this is how the Teacher in me teaches myself. I could unpack each paragraph to fill numerous pages, making it a larger book, but I do not wish to think for you. Rather, I desire for you to think for yourself; to learn to rely on your Soul to work with your psyche to unfold from within it what is right for you at the time. This way the book can be reread, each time gaining new insights from within; similar to the way some Master Teachers teach in parables or poems." ~ Stacey Stephens

Find all of the above offerings at SoulSelfLiving.com

About the Author

Stacey Stephens: Soul Awakener, Healer, Spiritual Teacher, Channel for The Ancient Ones & Bestselling Author

Stacey Stephens Co-Founded Soul Self Living, Inc. with her Soulmate and husband, Jack. For nearly 30 years she has assisted people as an energy healer. Since 2010, she has been channeling messages from The Ancient Ones and making them publicly available on the Soul Self Living website, in a weekly email to our subscribers, and collected by year as an Amazon Top 10 Bestselling Book Series, along with her paperback anthology Messages from The Ancient Ones: The First Five Years. These books are available on Amazon.com. She truly enjoys assisting people to uncover their purpose for this incarnation. Because her way of teaching is experiential, she has gained the reputation as a spiritual teacher who brings her students to a state of spiritual ecstasy through communion with their Divinity. Her purpose is to awaken humanity to the true understanding that we are all divine beings, capable of great acts, with everything we need to guide us toward fulfilling our missions.

About Soul Self Living

Jack and Stacey Stephens founded Soul Self Living with the intention to assist people to Awaken to the divine power within them, so they may co-create the life that fulfills their Soul's purpose for incarnating here on Earth.

To learn more, please visit www.SoulSelfLiving.com

www.ingramcontent.com/pod-product-compliance
Lightning Source LLC
LaVergne TN
LVHW051828080426
835512LV00018B/2780